Would You Build This?

A Story About the Firm You Would Design Today

MIKE GARRISON

ISBN: 9798986679334

Scriptor PUBLISHING GROUP

ScriptorPublishingGroup.com

Table of Contents

Foreword

I first met fellow speaker Mike Garrison in Charleston, South Carolina, one of those cities where history, hospitality, and high expectations all seem to collide. The room was filled with accomplished professionals at the Growth Drive Conference, the kind of people who know how to present well, speak carefully, and stay comfortably within the boundaries of what's expected.

And then there was Mike.

He didn't show up to impress the room. He showed up to wake it up.

What struck me first was how approachable he was, genuine, direct, and completely unfiltered. But it didn't take long to realize that behind that approachability was something much deeper: a man who has lived it, been burned by it, and come out the other side with a conviction he can't ignore.

This isn't theory for Mike.

This is earned.

When Mike and I spoke about this book, I could hear it in his voice, not just passion, but pain… and purpose. He's spent years investing time, money, and energy trying to help financial advisors and business owners do things the right way. And like many of us who operate as true fiduciaries, with a capital "F", he's seen firsthand how often the system doesn't reward that.

It rewards something else.

And that tension is what gave birth to this book.

At its core, *Would You Build This?* is not a strategy manual. It's not a playbook. It's not even a warning in the traditional sense.

It's a mirror.

I love that Mike chose to write this as a fable. Because if you are the right person, you won't just read it, you'll feel it. Through the story of David Carter, a successful advisor with a billion-dollar firm, strong margins, and everything "working," Mike invites you into a question that is both simple and deeply unsettling:

If you were starting today... would you build the firm you're currently running?

Not tweak it.

Not optimize it.

Would you build it?

One of the most powerful insights in this book is something many professionals feel but rarely articulate:

Not all revenue is created equally.

Some revenue is earned, through judgment, trust, and the kind of conversations that change the trajectory of a client's life.

Other revenue simply arrives, driven by markets, momentum, and systems that work whether you are deeply engaged or not.

On paper, they look identical.

But they are not.

And when you begin to see that difference, you can't unsee it.

Mike takes it a step further with a distinction that hit me hard:

Are you being received... or simply tolerated?

Some clients call you before they act. They seek your counsel. They trust your judgment.

Others call you after the decision is already made. They appreciate you, but they don't rely on you.

Both relationships generate revenue.

But they are not the same.

And yet, most firms, including very successful ones, are built in a way that doesn't distinguish between the two.

That's where the discomfort begins.

Now layer in what's happening around us.

We are entering a world where technology is removing opacity at a rate faster than most people realize. AI is not just improving efficiency, it's exposing truth.

And that truth is simple:

Clients are going to understand what they're paying... and why.

Mike said something to me that stuck:

"How you pay us is not what you pay us for."

That gap, the difference between perceived value and actual value, is where the tension lives.

And that tension is not going to fade.

It's going to accelerate.

I've lived through this before.

In the accounting industry, we've been experiencing this shift for the past decade. What started slowly, offshoring, retirements, private equity pressure, and increasing transparency, eventually compounded into a complete reshaping of the profession. And now, with generative AI, that change has moved into hyperdrive.

At first, it felt manageable.

Then it sped up.

And then, seemingly overnight, it was different.

That same wave is now forming in financial advisory.

Be careful.

It will feel slow... until it's not.

And when it hits, it won't just affect your firm, it will affect your clients, their expectations, and their willingness to question the value they receive.

Mike doesn't pretend to have all the answers.

In fact, one of the things I respect most about this book is that he openly admits that no one fully knows how this plays out.

But he does know this:

It is coming.

And there will be two types of firms on the other side.

- Those that lean fully into technology, scale, and efficiency, serving more clients at lower cost
- And those that lean fully into judgment, relationships, and deep value, operating more like a premium, high-trust advisory

Both can work.

But you can't pretend they're the same.

And you can't accidentally drift into one while believing you're building the other.

This book is written for a very specific person.

Not everyone.

It's written for the advisor who already feels it.

The one who's a little uncomfortable.

The one who senses that something isn't fully aligned but hasn't put language to it yet.

Mike told me this book is for "the ones who are worth everything they charge."

That matters.

Because this is not an attack on the profession.

It's a call to elevate it.

There's also something deeper running through this book that you can't ignore. Faith.

Not in a heavy-handed way, but in a foundational one.

This is a book about calling. About obedience. About having the courage to ask a question that could change everything, and then actually answer it.

Mike shared with me that when he finished writing this, he wept.

That tells you everything you need to know.

This isn't just a business decision.

This is a life decision.

That's why I invited Mike to speak at one of our exclusive 40 Strategy Growth Workshops.

He's a changemaker. He's passionate. And he's someone who has clearly been awakened to make a difference.

Some people will be energized by him immediately. Others may feel uncomfortable. He may ruffle some feathers. But I'm okay with that. Because if it wakes people up, if it gets them to think differently, act intentionally, and build something that actually aligns with what they believe, then it's worth it.

As you read this book, don't rush. Sit with it.

Let it challenge you.

Let it make you a little uncomfortable.

Because on the other side of that discomfort is clarity.

And on the other side of clarity… is choice.

And that choice will define your future.

So I'll leave you with the same question Mike is asking you:

If your value were fully transparent… would it hold?

And more importantly:

Would you build this?

— Carl J. Cox, CPA
CEO, 40 Strategy & 40 Accounting
Author, *Lost at CEO*
Host of the *Measure Success Podcast*

Prologue

The Moment Before It Changes

The room was quiet when the numbers appeared on the screen. No one at the table was inexperienced. The partners had built something substantial over decades—not through a single windfall or a fortunate market cycle, but through the slow, compounding discipline of showing up with competence and care. They had survived downturns that sent lesser firms scrambling. They had refined operations when refinement was unfashionable. They had recruited well, choosing character over credentials when the two diverged. They had navigated transitions that tested not only their strategy but their unity. The firm had crossed the billion-dollar mark in assets under management not through accident, but through consistency applied across years that no one was counting at the time.

The recap presentation was measured and professional. Liquidity would be meaningful. Infrastructure would strengthen. Growth would accelerate under institutional support. Governance would formalize. The language was not aggressive. It was prudent. Responsible. Mature. Every slide was designed to reassure, and every reassurance was grounded in something defensible.

Nothing in the presentation suggested instability.

That was what made the moment significant.

When firms are shrinking, when revenue is declining, when clients are leaving, decisions are forced. Pressure narrows options. Urgency simplifies analysis. In those moments, adaptation feels necessary—even inevitable. The mind sharpens because it has no choice.

But when everything is working—when margins are healthy, retention is strong, and valuation multiples are attractive—change is not required. It is chosen.

And chosen change reveals what you actually believe.

I have watched this moment arrive in firms across the country.

Over the past decade, the financial advisory profession has entered a new phase. Technology has isolated calculation. Portfolio construction is widely accessible. Planning software that once required teams and dedicated time can now generate projections in minutes. Fee transparency is increasing. Clients are more informed. Younger advisors are less patient with inherited assumptions, and less willing to build careers inside structures they had no hand in designing.

The surface of the profession still looks stable.

Beneath it, separation is underway.

Some firms are moving toward institutional scale. Private capital is entering the space more aggressively, bringing with it the rhythms and expectations of institutional ownership. Governance structures are tightening. Growth targets are becoming explicit. Enterprise value is being formalized in ways that previous generations of advisors never had to confront—or chose not to.

At the same time, clients are becoming more aware of what can be automated and what cannot. They can see what math costs. They can compare platforms. They can evaluate fees with increasing clarity.

And with that clarity comes a question they may not ask aloud but are certainly asking internally.

What they cannot replicate is judgment.

Judgment is not software. It is not performance reporting. It is not a projection output or a Monte Carlo simulation.

Judgment is the quiet conversation before a founder signs a document that will shape his family's future for a generation. It is the counsel that slows a liquidity event long enough to protect governance when everyone else in the room wants to move fast. It is the restraint that keeps success from distorting identity—the voice that says, "You can afford this, but that doesn't mean it serves you."

If that is what clients ultimately trust you for, then a deeper question emerges.

Does your firm reflect that?

For years, I have written and spoken about trust and judgment as the foundation of what we do. I have argued that when a client metaphorically hands you the keys to something valuable—their wealth, yes, but also their anxiety, their family dynamics, their sense of purpose—they are not buying an allocation model. They are extending belief. They are placing their future under your discernment, and that discernment carries a weight that no algorithm can bear.

But belief requires structure.

At some point, you must examine whether your compensation model, your growth assumptions, your referral posture, and your daily allocation of attention align with what you say you provide. Structure is not neutral. It either reinforces what you claim to value, or it quietly contradicts it.

I say this not from a distance. I have sat in the rooms where these conversations happen. I have watched partners weigh liquidity against legacy, growth against coherence, enterprise value against the quieter question of whether the thing they are building still resembles the thing they set out to build. And what I have come to understand is that the most important moment in a firm's life is not the moment of crisis. It is the moment of comfort—when everything is working well enough that you could justify changing nothing at all.

That is the moment this book is about.

The question that sits quietly beneath all of it is simple.

If you were starting today, would you build the firm you are currently running?

Not, would you tweak it.

Not, would you optimize it.

Would you build it.

That question is not an accusation. It is an invitation.

Many of you reading this book are successful. You have earned optionality. You have liquidity available. You have enterprise value that reflects years of disciplined work. You are not reacting to crisis. You are not retreating from failure.

You are standing at a moment where comfort and congruence are both available—and where having the space to think clearly about both is itself a gift.

This book is not about condemning scale or romanticizing independence. It is not a tactical manual for recap or rejection of it. It is not a marketing playbook or a polemic against institutional capital. And it is not a prescription. I have no interest in telling you what your firm should look like or what decision you should make.

It is a story about alignment.

It is a story about a successful advisor who discovers that the firm he has built faithfully over two decades is not the firm he would design in the environment he now faces. Not because the firm has failed him, but because he has grown past the assumptions on which it was built.

It is a story about courage that does not look dramatic from the outside—the kind of courage that shows up not as a bold gesture, but as a quiet refusal to let inertia substitute for intention.

And it is an invitation to build your own framework for thinking about what matters—before the pace of change accelerates and the space for reflection narrows.

Because the reality is this: the industry is shifting. Capital structures are evolving. Client expectations are rising. The advisors who navigate this well will not be the ones who reacted fastest. They will be the ones who thought most clearly—who took the time, early on, to ask themselves what they were building and why. Who examined their calling, their convictions, and their structure while there was still room to choose rather than to scramble.

That kind of early alignment does not limit your options.

It clarifies them.

And clarity, I have found, produces something rare in professional life.

Peace.

This book is my attempt to offer you the space for that reflection. What you do with it is yours.

Introduction

A Note Before the Story

The premise of this book can be stated simply.

If your clients trust you for judgment, the kind that cannot be automated, replicated, or reduced to a projection output, then the structure of your firm should make that obvious. Your compensation model, your growth assumptions, your referral posture, and the way you allocate your daily attention should all reflect the thing you say you provide. The structure is not neutral. It either reinforces what you claim to value, or it quietly contradicts it.

That alignment, or the lack of it, is what this book is about.

I use the word alignment deliberately, and I will use it often. You may also hear congruence, and I intend the same meaning: the state in which what you believe, what you practice, and what your structure rewards all point in the same direction. When they diverge, when the firm you are running no longer resembles the firm you would design, something essential is lost, even when the numbers look strong. Especially when the numbers look strong.

To explore this idea, I have chosen to tell a story.

The chapters that follow are built around a fictional character named David Carter: a senior financial advisor and partner at a successful firm called Northbridge Financial. David is not a single person

I have known. He is a composite, drawn from years of conversations with advisors across the country who have found themselves standing in the kind of tension this book describes: the tension between a firm that is working and a conviction that it could be built differently.

David's colleagues, clients, and mentors are also fictional, though many of their conversations are grounded in real exchanges I have witnessed or participated in. You will meet Michael, the managing partner whose institutional vision for Northbridge is rational and well-intentioned. Rachel, a trusted colleague whose loyalty and perceptiveness accompany David into the next chapter of his career. Matt, a client and friend whose pointed question on a river one morning helps David name what he has been feeling. Harry, a retired advisor whose hard-won wisdom arrives without agenda. Claire, David's wife, whose quiet intelligence and steady presence anchor him when the ground shifts. And Thomas, a craftsman whose understanding of integrity in work becomes an unexpected mirror for David's own journey.

I chose a parable rather than a prescriptive framework because I believe the most important ideas in our profession are not absorbed through argument. They are recognized. A good story allows you to experience someone else's thinking in real time, to sit inside the doubt, the clarity, and the cost of aligning conviction with structure. My hope is that as you follow David's journey, you will find yourself nodding at certain moments, not because his situation is identical to yours, but because the underlying question is the same.

One more thing before you begin.

My convictions about this work are not merely strategic. They are rooted in my faith in Jesus Christ. I believe that what we do as advisors is stewardship, that the trust clients extend to us carries a weight that is ultimately spiritual, not just professional. That belief shapes how I think about compensation, about growth, about courage, and about what it means to build something that endures. You will see this perspective surface in the story, and more directly in the final chapter.

I share this not to narrow the audience but to be honest about the foundation. The principles in this book, alignment, discernment, the courage to build from conviction rather than convenience, are ones I believe apply broadly, regardless of how you articulate your own foundation. What matters is that you have one, and that you are willing to let it shape your structure, not just your marketing.

This book is not a prescription. It does not tell you what your firm should look like or what decision you should make. It is an invitation to sit with a question that, once honestly formed, rarely disappears:

If you were starting today, would you build the firm you are currently running?

What you do with that question is yours.

But I believe you deserve the space to ask it clearly, before the pace of change narrows your options.

That is what the pages ahead are for.

Chapter 1

The Numbers Were Right

David Carter had reviewed year-end numbers for nearly 20 years, and most years the ritual carried a quiet satisfaction. January had always been his season for this—the office still carrying the hush of the holidays, the new calendar unmarked, the previous year's performance reduced to columns that either confirmed or corrected what intuition had suggested. There was something reassuring about disciplined growth—the steady accumulation of assets, the incremental improvement of margins, the compounding effect of relationships built carefully over time. Northbridge Financial had not grown by accident. It had grown by intention, restraint, and a kind of professional conservatism that rewarded patience more than flair. It was the sort of firm that clients described by saying, "They've never given me a reason to leave." That was not a dramatic endorsement. It was a durable one.

The firm occupied the top floor of a downtown building that conveyed permanence without extravagance. Clients stepped out of the elevator into a reception area framed in glass and warm wood, the skyline visible but not imposing. The conference rooms were thoughtfully designed, neither ostentatious nor austere. When David walked through the office in the early morning before anyone else arrived, he often felt a quiet pride in what they had built. It was substantial. It was disciplined. It was respected. And on mornings like this one—when the light came through the eastern windows and the silence still held—it felt like something that would last.

This year's numbers were strong.

Assets under management had crossed the billion-dollar threshold—a milestone that had once seemed distant and almost theoretical. Revenue per advisor had increased modestly. Client retention remained above 96 percent. Recruiting conversations were active. Operational expenses had been controlled without eroding service. Markets had cooperated. By every conventional measure, the firm was performing exactly as a well-run advisory practice should.

Nothing in the spreadsheet suggested instability.

Michael sat at the head of the conference table during the annual review meeting, moving through the recap materials with steady confidence. He was not theatrical, but he was precise. He believed in disciplined growth and saw recapitalization as a natural evolution for firms that had reached their scale. Liquidity would strengthen the partners personally. Outside capital would accelerate recruiting. Governance structure would formalize what they had already built informally. His conviction was not aggressive. It was architectural—he saw recap as the next floor of a building that already had a sound foundation.

"Margin expansion came in ahead of projection," Michael said, tapping the page lightly with his pen. "Operational leverage is working."

Heads nodded around the table.

David nodded as well.

He had advocated for much of that operational leverage. Centralized planning support. Workflow refinement. Tighter review cycles. He believed in building durable systems that did not depend on heroics. The firm's growth was not accidental. It was engineered. And he took a craftsman's satisfaction in the fact that the machinery ran quietly—that clients experienced quality without ever seeing the structure behind it.

And yet, as the discussion moved deeper into revenue attribution, his attention lingered on a smaller figure buried halfway down the page—advisory revenue attributable to market appreciation versus revenue generated through new planning engagements and expanded advisory scope.

The percentage had shifted.

Markets had done more of the work this year.

It was not alarming. It was not even unusual. In a strong market cycle, asset-based revenue naturally expanded. That was the stability the model promised. Clients benefited from growth. The firm participated proportionally. Everyone understood the structure. No one at the table would have flagged the number as a concern.

Still, the number held his attention longer than it should have.

There was a distinction David had learned to notice over two decades of practice—the difference between revenue that was earned and revenue that arrived. Both showed up on the same line. Both supported the same payroll and the same overhead. But they carried different weight. Revenue earned through deeper engagement, through planning conversations that changed how a client thought about their future, through the kind of counsel that required preparation and judgment—that revenue meant the client needed you specifically. Revenue that arrived because markets rose meant the client needed a structure. Any structure.

"What are you seeing?" Michael asked when he noticed David studying the page.

"Just mix," David replied. "Market contribution versus planning."

Michael shrugged slightly. "It evens out over cycles."

"Yes," David said.

He did not disagree. Over decades, markets corrected and recovered. Asset-based revenue stabilized through volatility. The structure had proven resilient through multiple cycles. Michael was not wrong about the math.

But as recap projections appeared on the screen—liquidity distributions, governance adjustments, growth targets required to justify valuation—the question surfaced quietly, without drama.

If I were starting today, would I build this?

He did not mean Northbridge itself. He did not regret the years invested. He did not question the integrity of the partners or the discipline of the firm. They had built something strong. They had served clients faithfully. They had navigated downturns and expansion without recklessness.

He meant the structure.

If a younger version of himself entered the profession today—an environment where planning software could generate projections in seconds, where fee transparency was increasing, where clients compared advisory value more openly—would he design a compensation model that leaned so naturally on market appreciation?

Would he bundle judgment and exposure in the same way?

The meeting adjourned without tension. Partners gathered their materials, exchanged brief comments about recruiting targets, and returned to offices that bore their names on frosted glass panels. The skyline beyond the windows looked unchanged, steady in the late afternoon light. Someone down the hall laughed about a weekend plan. A phone rang and was answered on the second ring. The ordinary sounds of a firm that was functioning exactly as it was designed to function.

David remained seated for a moment longer after the others left.

He closed the recap packet and rested his hands on the table.

The numbers were right.

That was what unsettled him.

If something had been broken—if margins were compressing, if clients were leaving, if markets had exposed structural weakness—the decision-making would have been straightforward. Problems invite correction. The mind knows what to do with a deficit. It mobilizes. It focuses. It repairs.

But nothing was visibly wrong.

The firm was profitable. Clients were satisfied. Partners were aligned around growth.

And yet the question persisted.

If I were starting today, would I build this?

It was not a rebellious thought. It did not carry anger or dissatisfaction. It carried responsibility. Structure shapes behavior. He had taught that principle to younger advisors for years. Compensation systems influence decision-making. Growth assumptions determine posture. Incentives quietly direct attention. He had said all of this in training sessions and partner retreats, and he had believed it each time. The question now was whether he believed it enough to apply it to himself.

If clients ultimately trusted him for judgment—the kind of judgment that kept a founder from conceding leverage late at night when fatigue tempted compromise—then perhaps the structure should make that clearer. Perhaps the way the firm earned its revenue should reflect, more precisely, the thing the firm was actually trusted to provide.

He stood and walked slowly to the window.

The city below moved with predictable rhythm. Traffic lights shifted. Pedestrians crossed at measured intervals. Nothing signaled disruption. The world outside the glass had no awareness of the question forming inside it.

From the outside, Northbridge looked exactly as it should.

From the inside, something had shifted.

Not a crisis.

A question.

And questions, he knew from experience, rarely disappear once they are fully formed.

Chapter 2

The Question in the Current

For several days after the partner meeting, David carried the question without speaking it aloud.

It accompanied him in small, ordinary moments. While reviewing client files in the early morning before the office filled with voices and routine. While driving home through familiar traffic patterns he could navigate almost without attention, his hands steady on the wheel, his mind somewhere else entirely. While standing in the kitchen, rinsing a glass and listening to the low hum of the refrigerator after Claire had gone upstairs. The question did not announce itself. It simply remained—present the way a low-grade awareness of weather is present, shaping what you notice without demanding that you act.

He did not feel agitation. He did not feel anger. He felt awareness.

If I were starting today, would I build this?

He tested the question against different angles, as if rotating a stone in his hand to see how the light struck each facet. Was it ego? A desire to differentiate himself from Michael and the other partners? Fatigue after two decades of leadership—the kind that masquerades as restlessness? He dismissed each possibility in turn, not because he was incapable of ego or fatigue, but because neither explained the steadiness of the thought. It did not flare and recede the way dissatisfaction does. It persisted. It had the quality of something that had been true for longer than he had been willing to notice.

He found himself watching client behavior more closely that week. Which clients called before acting, and which called after decisions had already been made? Which invited counsel early—when options were still open and direction still malleable—and which sought confirmation once risk had already been assumed? The distinction mattered to David. It represented two fundamentally different relationships with advisory value. And yet the structure rewarded both equally. The revenue arrived the same way, regardless of posture. A client who leaned on David's judgment at the most consequential moments of a transition generated the same fee as a client who needed only periodic rebalancing and an annual review.

The observation was not accusatory. It was clarifying.

By Friday afternoon, the question had settled into something less abstract. It was no longer simply about recap or valuation or even the partner meeting that had triggered it. It was about design. About whether the model that had supported two decades of faithful work was the one he would deliberately choose in an environment where judgment stood apart from calculation more clearly than ever before. The profession had changed around him—not suddenly, not dramatically, but with the slow certainty of a tide—and the structure he operated within had not changed with it.

That weekend, he and Matt Hendricks drove north before sunrise. Matt had been David's client for nearly a decade—first through the sale of his manufacturing company, then through the liquidity and governance decisions that followed. But somewhere in the late nights and difficult conversations that surround a founder's transition, the relationship had crossed from professional to personal. They fished together each spring because they had earned the right to stand in a river without needing to explain why they were there. This March the banks were exposed in places that normally sat beneath moving water, and the current revealed more of the rocks beneath its surface. David noticed it as soon as they stepped out of the truck. The landscape looked the same from a distance—the same tree line, the same bend in the water, the same gravel path from the road—but the river itself had receded enough to expose what was usually hidden.

"Levels are down," Matt said, tightening the straps on his waders.

"They are," David replied.

Matt moved into the river first, testing the footing with deliberate care. He had always fished the way he ran his company before selling it—patiently, aware of undercurrents, attentive to force beneath surface calm. He was the kind of man who trusted his own perception but verified it with his feet before committing his weight. David followed, placing each step with similar caution. The water was cold enough to sharpen attention, and the uneven bottom required the kind of focus that left no room for anything else.

They stood in silence for several minutes, casting upstream and letting their lines drift naturally with the current. The rhythm of the river demanded attention. There was no room for distracted thought once the fly hit the water. That was part of why David valued these mornings. The river did not allow multitasking. It required you to be exactly where you were.

Eventually, Matt broke the quiet.

"You ever look at those new planning tools?" he asked, eyes still tracking the drift of his line.

"I've seen a few," David said.

"Thirty or forty bucks a month," Matt continued. "Plug in assumptions, get projections. Clean output."

"They're improving," David acknowledged.

Matt reeled in slowly and cast again.

"So what's the difference?" he asked.

"Between what?" David replied.

"Between that," Matt said, nodding vaguely toward the imagined laptop on the riverbank, "and what you do."

The question was not confrontational. It carried curiosity, not skepticism. Matt was not testing David. He was thinking out loud—the way a man does when he trusts the person beside him enough to let an unfinished thought leave his mouth.

David did not answer immediately. He let his line drift past a submerged rock before retrieving it. The silence between them was not uncomfortable. It was the kind of silence that exists between two people who have spent enough time together to know that an answer worth giving sometimes needs a moment to find its shape.

"Projection is math," he said at last. "What I do is sequence decisions."

Matt glanced sideways at him.

"Meaning?"

"Meaning knowing when not to optimize," David replied. "Meaning understanding how liquidity changes family dynamics. Meaning telling you not to concede language in a deal when you're tired."

A faint smile crossed Matt's face.

"You didn't manage the math that night," he said. "You protected me from myself."

David said nothing. The memory was vivid enough without elaboration—a late-night call, a deal term that looked reasonable on paper but would have shifted leverage in ways Matt would have regretted for years. David had been the voice that said stop. Not because the math was wrong, but because the timing was.

They stood in the current for another moment before Matt added, "That wasn't a model. That was judgment."

"Yes," David said.

Matt shifted his footing and looked at him more directly.

"If what I'm paying you for is judgment," he said evenly, "then the way I pay you should make that obvious."

The line drifted farther downstream than David intended before he noticed it.

He reeled it in slowly.

He had heard versions of that question before, usually framed as fee compression or technology disruption—the kind of challenge that arrives in industry panels and trade publications, abstract enough to acknowledge and move past. This was different. It was not about price. It was about clarity. It was a client—a client who trusted him deeply—telling him that the way value was exchanged between them did not match the value itself.

"If it's judgment," Matt continued, "then structure should reflect that."

The river moved steadily around them. A bird called from somewhere upstream and was answered from the far bank. The morning light had shifted from gray to gold without either of them marking the transition.

David felt the earlier question resurface with greater weight now, no longer abstract and no longer solitary. It had been spoken—not by him, but by the person whose trust made the question impossible to dismiss.

If I were starting today, would I build this?

For the first time, he realized the question might not be about growth at all.

It might be about alignment.

Chapter 3

Accumulation

David did not announce that he was reviewing the firm's referral patterns.

He simply asked Rachel for five years of data. The request came on a Monday in mid-March, with the last of winter's gray still holding outside the office windows. Rachel had joined Northbridge as an operations associate a decade earlier and had risen to become the firm's director of client operations—the person who held the infrastructure together while the partners held the relationships.

She did not question the request. Over the years, she had learned to distinguish between curiosity and direction. When David asked for historical information with that particular tone—quiet, specific, and without explanation—it meant he was tracing something structural. Rachel had been with the firm long enough to recognize the difference between a partner looking for confirmation and a partner looking for truth. This was the latter.

Two days later she entered his office carrying a thick binder and a spreadsheet printed on oversized legal paper. The late afternoon light slanted through the glass wall behind her, catching faint dust in the air. David cleared a space on his desk without being asked, moving aside a framed photo of Claire and a cup of coffee that had gone cold hours ago.

"Outbound first?" she asked.

"Yes," he said.

They sat across from one another at his desk. The office was quiet. Most of the staff had already left for the day. Through the glass wall, the hallway lights had dimmed to their evening setting, and the only sound was the low hum of the building's ventilation system—the kind of background noise you stop hearing until silence makes you notice it again.

Rachel opened the binder and turned to the first tab. The pattern was predictable.

Estate planning attorneys. Two primary CPAs. A valuation firm. The same names appeared repeatedly across the years. The relationships were longstanding and competent. The professionals were reliable. Clients benefited from coordination. It was the kind of professional ecosystem that develops naturally around a firm of Northbridge's size and tenure—a constellation of trusted advisors who referred to one another because they had worked together long enough to know what to expect.

There was nothing negligent in it.

If a client needed estate documents, they called Attorney A. If a complex tax question arose, they involved CPA B. If a business sale was on the horizon, they reached out to the valuation firm they had known for a decade. The process was smooth. The outcomes were generally good. No client had ever complained about the quality of a referral.

It was efficient.

It was also automatic.

David traced the names slowly with his finger. He was not looking for failures. He was looking for something subtler—the difference between a system that had been designed and a system that had simply accreted. These referral patterns had not been chosen through deliberate evaluation. They had formed the way riverbeds form—through repetition, through the path of least resistance, through the quiet accumulation of habit over years.

The volume of referrals outward was consistent and generous. Northbridge had been a good partner to the professionals in its orbit. They had shared business freely when client needs required it. David had always believed in generosity of referral. It was, he felt, a mark of professional maturity—a willingness to direct a client toward the best resource, even when that resource existed outside your own walls.

"Now inbound," he said.

Rachel turned the page.

The numbers were respectable. Some years stronger than others. But the sources were inconsistent.

A client introduced a sibling unexpectedly. A founder mentioned David at dinner and a phone call followed. A CPA referred a cousin who had just inherited money and didn't know where to start. A business owner brought a friend to a review meeting without warning, and the friend became a client within the quarter.

The firm grew.

But it did not design growth.

Over five years, Northbridge had referred significantly more measurable business outward than it had received back in structured revenue. That imbalance was not inherently problematic—collaboration was not a ledger to be balanced, and David had never believed in keeping score with professional partners. Still, the data revealed something about how growth arrived. It arrived the way weather arrives. You could observe it. You could benefit from it. But you could not claim to have caused it.

It arrived through weather.

Market appreciation.

Unpredictable introductions.

Recruiting momentum.

It did not arrive through a deliberate, cultivated system of aligned relationships.

"We project growth confidently," David said quietly, still studying the spreadsheet, "but we don't engineer it."

Rachel looked at him carefully. She had the kind of intelligence that processed what was said alongside what was meant, and she rarely confused the two.

"You're not saying it's weak," she said.

"No," he replied.

"You're saying it's assumed."

"Yes."

He leaned back in his chair and let the observation settle. The ceiling above him was unremarkable—standard commercial tile, recessed lighting—but he stared at it the way a person stares at a ceiling when they are not looking at the ceiling at all.

Northbridge rewarded accumulation.

That was the core of it.

The structure was built around asset growth. Revenue expanded as assets expanded. Clients who increased exposure generated proportional growth for the firm. That was the design. It was transparent and widely accepted. It was, in fact, the dominant model across the industry—so common that questioning it felt almost impolite, like questioning the foundation of a building while standing inside it.

But the model did not differentiate between depth and exposure.

A client who invited counsel early, who sought advice before making decisions, who relied on judgment to navigate complexity—who called at ten o'clock at night because a deal term didn't feel right and they trusted David enough to say so—generated the same recurring revenue as a client who simply parked assets and called after decisions were already made.

The compensation model did not distinguish between being received and being tolerated.

It bundled them.

That evening, after dinner, Claire found him still seated at the kitchen table with the printed spreadsheet in front of him. The dishes had been cleared. The house was quiet in the particular way it becomes quiet when children have grown and the evening belongs entirely to two people who have learned to share silence comfortably.

"You're not worried," she said.

"No."

"Then what are you?"

He looked up at her.

"Unsettled."

She sat across from him. She did not reach for the spreadsheet or ask what the numbers meant. Claire had never involved herself in the operational details of the firm, but she had an unerring sense for when David was processing something that mattered—and she knew that what he needed in those moments was not analysis but presence.

"For 20 years," he said slowly, "I've told younger advisors that structure shapes behavior more than talent does. That incentives quietly direct attention. That compensation influences posture."

"You still believe that," she said.

"I do."

He slid the spreadsheet slightly toward her, though she did not read it.

"But what if the structure that helped us grow isn't the one I would design now?"

Claire studied his expression. There was no panic in it. No resentment. What she saw was the face of a man who had discovered a misalignment between what he practiced and what he preached—and who took that misalignment seriously enough to sit with it rather than explain it away.

"This isn't about money," she said.

"No."

"It's about congruence."

He nodded.

If clients ultimately trusted him for judgment—the kind that kept a founder from conceding leverage late at night when fatigue clouded clarity—then the way the firm was compensated should reflect that explicitly. The fee should not arrive as a byproduct of market movement. It should arrive as a direct exchange for the thing the client actually valued.

If growth mattered, it should be cultivated intentionally, not inherited accidentally.

If referrals mattered, they should be structured around alignment rather than habit.

He ran his hand across the edge of the table—a gesture Claire recognized. It was what he did when a thought had finished forming and he was preparing to say it aloud for the first time.

"If I were starting today," he said quietly, "I'm not sure I would build it this way."

Claire did not rush to reassure him. That was one of the things he valued most about her—she did not treat uncertainty as something to be solved. She treated it as something to be respected.

"That's not rebellion," she said.

"No."

"It's stewardship."

The word lingered long after they turned out the lights.

Chapter 4

Four Columns

Recap discussions did not erupt into urgency overnight. They gathered momentum gradually, like pressure building beneath an otherwise stable surface. No single event forced the conversation. No crisis accelerated the timeline. It was more like a season changing—imperceptible from day to day, unmistakable over weeks.

The formal indication of interest arrived on a Tuesday morning in early April. The email was professional and restrained. The Chicago firm positioned itself as a partner rather than an acquirer. Minority stake. Preserved leadership. Accelerated growth. Liquidity without displacement. It was written in language designed to reduce fear—every sentence calibrated to make the reader feel that saying yes was the prudent thing, the mature thing, the thing that serious people do when they reach this stage.

Michael forwarded the document to the partners with a short message: "Worth serious discussion."

The next partner meeting extended longer than usual. A banker appeared on screen precisely at nine, his tone steady and analytical. He did not oversell. He did not dramatize. He spoke in ratios and timelines. His presentation had the polished confidence of a man who had delivered it dozens of times to firms that looked exactly like

Northbridge—firms that had done the hard work of building something real and now stood at the threshold of monetizing it.

"We partner with firms that are already disciplined," he said. "We don't fix broken ones."

He outlined operational leverage, centralized planning support, recruiting acceleration, and margin expansion achieved through scale. He spoke about optionality, about institutional stability, about the kind of structure that made firms resilient over decades rather than dependent on individual principals. Every point was supported by data. Every projection was grounded in comparable transactions.

"Our data shows consistent expansion within 18 months," he said.

Slides advanced methodically across the screen. Valuation multiples were competitive. Liquidity numbers were not theoretical; they were specific. Governance adjustments were clearly defined. The presentation was, in its way, a mirror—showing each partner a version of themselves that was wealthier, more secure, and more institutionally supported than the version sitting in the room.

Nothing in the presentation felt reckless.

When the banker signed off, the room remained quiet for a moment—not because of doubt, but because of calculation. Each partner was doing private arithmetic, translating multiples into mortgages paid off, college funds secured, estate plans simplified.

"This protects what we've built," one partner said.

"It gives us flexibility," another added.

Michael leaned back slightly and folded his hands. He had the expression of a man who had anticipated this moment and prepared for it—not with manipulation, but with the steady conviction that institutional partnership was the logical next step for a firm of their caliber.

"We've reached a size where this makes sense," he said. "If we don't move deliberately, we leave value on the table."

No one disagreed outright.

David did not disagree either.

He had guided clients through recapitalizations before. He understood the logic. He respected capital when deployed with discipline. He knew that liquidity could strengthen families and reduce risk. He knew that scale could create opportunity. He had seen it work well and he had seen it work poorly, and he understood that the difference was almost always in the character of the people involved rather than the structure of the deal.

But as the discussion turned toward timing—closing before year-end to optimize tax treatment, formalizing governance transitions, aligning recruiting incentives—he felt something more definitive than before.

Recap would not merely strengthen Northbridge.

It would formalize direction.

Growth would no longer be assumed; it would be required. Productivity would be measured against defined benchmarks. Infrastructure would tighten around explicit expectations. The firm would become accountable to a partner whose definition of success was expressed in growth rates and margin targets—metrics that were not wrong, exactly, but that did not capture everything David believed the firm was for.

The meeting adjourned with action items and follow-up calls scheduled.

Driving home that evening, David recalculated his personal liquidity projection in his mind. The numbers were substantial. More than sufficient. Enough to eliminate financial uncertainty for the rest of his life. Enough to simplify estate planning. Enough to create a margin of comfort he had never known in his early years building the firm, when cash flow was uncertain and every new client felt like oxygen. He had earned this. Twenty years of discipline had produced real, tangible value. No one could question that.

At dinner, he laid the numbers out plainly for Claire.

"If we recap before year-end," he said, "tax treatment improves. Liquidity is significant."

Claire listened without interruption. She had a way of holding silence that was not passive but attentive—the silence of a person who understands that the first thing someone says is rarely the thing they actually need to talk about.

"Would it secure us?" she asked.

"Yes."

"Would it secure the firm?"

"Yes."

She paused.

"Would it secure alignment?"

He hesitated.

"I don't know."

That was the first honest fracture.

Recap would secure comfort. It would secure structure. It would secure predictability. It would answer every question a financial planner would ask about a client in David's position. And yet David was not his own client. He was the advisor, and the advisor's question was different. The advisor's question was not "Is this sufficient?" but "Is this congruent?"

It might not secure congruence.

Later that night, after Claire had gone upstairs, David returned to the kitchen table with a blank legal pad. The house was quiet except for the low hum of the refrigerator and the occasional passing car outside. The kitchen light cast a warm circle on the table, and beyond it the room receded into shadow. It was the kind of solitude he had always done his clearest thinking in—late, alone, with nothing competing for his attention.

He drew four columns.

Recap. Optimize. Stay. Separate.

He stared at the headings for a long moment before writing beneath them.

Recap offered clarity of a certain kind. Liquidity. Infrastructure. Accelerated growth. Reduced personal risk. It would quiet any external speculation. It would signal prudence. It would make the next decade measurable. It was the column that required the least explanation—the one that every industry peer, every banker, every conference speaker would affirm without hesitation.

Optimize required no capital partner. Northbridge could raise minimums, refine client segmentation, increase revenue per household, and tighten internal operations. It preserved autonomy. It allowed incremental adjustment without structural overhaul. But it also preserved the underlying architecture that David had begun to question—the bundling of judgment and exposure, the compensation model that could not distinguish between depth and convenience.

Stay required the least disruption. Let recap pass. Trust incremental improvement. Revisit alignment later. There was comfort in deferral. There was safety in waiting. And there was precedent—how many advisors had asked themselves this same question and concluded, reasonably, that the moment was not right, that conditions would improve, that the discomfort would pass? David knew the answer. Most of them. And most of them were still waiting.

Separate was the only column that did not promise reinforcement.

It required selling equity independently. Leaving a firm he had helped build for 20 years. Explaining to clients why he was stepping away at a moment when most peers would double down. Starting again without inherited pipeline or weather-driven growth. It was the column that would look, from the outside, like the least rational choice—the one that defied every conventional metric of professional success.

He considered Rachel. Ten years of operational partnership. Shared trust with clients. A professional life structured around stability and competence. She had built her career inside Northbridge with the same quiet discipline David admired. Would he ask her to follow? Would it be fair to present that option, knowing the weight it carried?

No.

He had already decided that much.

He would not recruit. If Rachel chose to come, it would be because she saw what he saw—not because he had persuaded her. The decision had to be hers, fully and freely, or it would carry a debt that neither of them could afford.

He considered the younger advisors inside Northbridge who were building books under the firm's banner. Would his departure destabilize them? Would it fracture perception? Would it complicate recap timing in ways that felt selfish? He owed them honesty. He owed them a transition that did not diminish what they had built. Whatever he decided, it could not be at their expense.

He forced himself to follow each column forward honestly.

Recap preserved comfort now and direction later.

Optimize preserved familiarity.

Stay preserved reputation.

Separate preserved congruence.

He set the pen down.

The question was no longer abstract.

It was not about dissatisfaction. It was not about ego. It was not about ambition or restlessness or the romantic appeal of starting over.

It was about whether the structure he was preparing to formalize reflected what he believed he actually provided. Whether the thing he had spent 20 years building would, if formalized under institutional capital, become more of what it should be—or more of what was already misaligned.

He closed his eyes and let the quiet stretch.

Comfort now.

Or clarity now.

Upstairs, Claire moved lightly across the floor. The sound was faint—barely audible through the ceiling—but David heard it the way a person hears the movements of someone they have loved for a long time: without needing to interpret it.

He folded the legal pad closed and turned off the kitchen light.

The columns did not resolve themselves that night.

But for the first time, he understood the cost of each.

Chapter 5

Before the Room Filled

David arrived earlier than usual that morning. The conference had fallen in late April this year, and the drive to the hotel had carried him through streets where dogwoods were just reaching full bloom—white and pink against the still-bare upper canopy of the oaks.

The hotel ballroom was only half arranged when he stepped inside. Round tables stood draped in white linen, some with chairs still stacked beside them. A staff member adjusted a microphone stand near the small stage. Coffee urns steamed quietly along the back wall, filling the room with the faint, familiar scent of burnt beans and carpet. Name badges were fanned across a registration table near the entrance, each one representing a firm, a career, a version of the same professional life David had been living for two decades.

He preferred arriving before the room filled. It gave him space to observe without performing. He could stand near the windows, cup in hand, and gather himself before the rhythm of conversation began. These industry events had become predictable in their cadence—the same growth language, the same recruiting concerns, the same cautious optimism about markets and margins. He attended because the relationships mattered. But increasingly, the conversations felt like they were circling the same center without ever reaching it.

He poured coffee and moved toward the glass overlooking the street below. The city was just beginning to animate—delivery trucks backing into narrow alleys, early commuters stepping briskly along the sidewalk, lights turning green in steady sequence. From up here, the patterns looked orderly. Everything moved along its designated path.

The question had not left him.

If I were starting today, would I build this?

He had not said it aloud to anyone but Claire. He had not framed it as dissent. He had not allowed it to influence his tone at the office or his demeanor at partner meetings. But it followed him here, even into rooms where growth strategies and leadership themes were the expected topics. It was becoming less a question he asked himself and more a lens through which he saw everything—every conversation about scale, every assumption about what success required, every projection that treated growth as the natural measure of health.

"Mind if I join you?"

The voice came from his left, measured and unhurried.

David turned. The man who had spoken appeared to be in his late sixties, well-dressed but without display. His suit was charcoal, well-fitted, unremarkable. His shoes were clean but not new. Nothing about his appearance asked to be noticed. But his posture carried a kind of steadiness that did not require introduction—the bearing of a man who had earned the right to move slowly and was no longer interested in proving anything to anyone.

"Of course," David said.

They shook hands.

"Harry Lawson."

"David Carter."

They began with ordinary conversation—regional growth trends, leadership fatigue in mid-market firms, the changing expectations of younger professionals who wanted flexibility and purpose in measures their predecessors had not demanded. Harry listened more than he spoke, and when he did speak, his tone was precise rather than expansive. He did not offer opinions so much as observations, and each one carried the weight of having been tested against experience before being spoken aloud.

"How long have you been building your firm?" Harry asked.

"Twenty years."

Harry nodded slowly. Not in acknowledgment of the number, but as if in recognition of what two decades of building required—the decisions absorbed, the seasons endured, the quiet erosion of certainty that comes from doing anything long enough to see its limitations.

"And if you were starting today," he asked evenly, "would you build it the same way?"

The question struck with such familiarity that David felt an almost physical reaction—a stillness that moved through his chest and settled in his hands. It was the same question he had been carrying for weeks, spoken now by a stranger as casually as if he were asking about the coffee.

He did not answer immediately.

Harry did not press.

Around them, the ballroom gradually filled. Chairs scraped lightly across carpet. Low conversations overlapped. A waiter passed carrying a tray of pastries. The room was assembling itself into the shape of an event—the familiar choreography of professionals preparing to be spoken to.

"It's a simple question," Harry continued gently, "but most successful men dislike it."

"Why?" David asked.

"Because it forces separation between what has worked in the past and what now aligns. Those are not the same thing, and admitting that feels like ingratitude. You built something that succeeded. To question whether you would build it again can feel like dishonoring the years that produced it."

David studied him. There was no salesmanship in Harry's manner. No agenda behind the words. He spoke the way a man speaks when he has already made his own difficult decisions and has no interest in being validated for them—only in being honest about what they cost.

"We're considering recapitalization," David said after a moment. "Liquidity. Governance structure. Accelerated growth."

Harry did not react with surprise or approval.

"And?" he asked.

"If I were starting today," David said slowly, "I'm not sure I would design it that way."

Harry stirred his coffee once, thoughtfully. The spoon made a quiet sound against the ceramic—small and precise, like punctuation at the end of a sentence.

"Do you know Luke 10?" he asked.

David nodded. He did.

"When Christ sent the 72 out," Harry said quietly, "He didn't tell them to build scale. He didn't tell them to secure territory. He didn't tell them to establish institutions or measure productivity. He told them to enter a town, speak peace, and look for a person of peace—someone who would receive them. And to stay there."

The noise in the room continued to rise around them, but their conversation seemed oddly insulated from it—two men standing near a window, speaking in low voices about something that had nothing and everything to do with business.

"You can build scale where you're tolerated," Harry said, his voice still even, "or depth where you're received."

David felt the sentence settle. It did not land like an argument. It landed like a diagnosis—precise, quiet, and impossible to un-feel once it had been spoken.

He had built scale. He had built discipline. He had built something substantial. The evidence was in the spreadsheets, in the retention numbers, in the billion-dollar milestone that everyone at Northbridge was rightly proud of.

But had he built where he was received?

Or where he was simply effective?

The distinction was not one he had ever been asked to make. Effectiveness was the standard the profession measured by. Client retention, revenue growth, operational efficiency—these were the metrics that defined success. No conference speaker had ever taken the stage to ask whether you were building where you were received. The question belonged to a different vocabulary entirely—one that David recognized from a part of his life he did not often bring into professional conversations.

"Stop asking what works," Harry continued. "Start asking what aligns."

There was no accusation in his tone. No dramatic emphasis. The statement did not seek to provoke; it sought to clarify. And it clarified something David had been circling for weeks without being able to name: the difference between a firm that functioned well and a firm that reflected what its founder actually believed.

The program began shortly afterward. A speaker took the stage and began discussing leadership resilience in uncertain markets. Applause followed key phrases. Laughter rose at familiar anecdotes. Slides advanced. Pens moved across notepads. The room performed its role with practiced ease.

David heard almost none of it.

The phrase repeated quietly in his mind.

Build where you are received.

Stay there.

For the first time, the question about recap felt less like strategy and more like obedience. Not obedience to a market condition or a business imperative, but to something deeper—a conviction about what his work was actually for, and whether the structure he was preparing to formalize would honor that conviction or quietly bury it beneath the language of growth.

He did not know what that obedience required yet.

But he knew the question would not leave him alone.

Chapter 6

Filtering

David did not announce a philosophical shift at Northbridge. He did not schedule a strategy session or circulate a memo. He did not raise the question at a partner meeting or invite outside counsel to evaluate the firm's direction. Nothing in his outward behavior signaled that anything had changed.

He observed.

The habit began almost unconsciously, the way a musician begins hearing things in a piece of music that a casual listener would never notice. In meetings, he paid closer attention to posture than to performance. Which clients invited counsel before acting, and which sought affirmation after decisions were already in motion? Which conversations began with uncertainty—genuine, unguarded uncertainty—and which began with conclusions already reached, the meeting serving only to confirm what the client had already decided to do?

He had always noticed these differences. But he had never organized them. Now he did.

One afternoon, a long-time client mentioned casually that he had committed capital to a private investment introduced by a friend. The conversation was friendly. The client was in good spirits. He described the opportunity with the particular enthusiasm of a man who believed he had discovered something ahead of the crowd.

"When did that happen?" David asked, keeping his tone even.

"About a month ago," the client replied. "I figured we'd talk through allocation adjustments at the next review."

The investment was not reckless. It was not fraudulent. The client had not violated any agreement or acted with malice. But the commitment introduced complexity that now required coordination after the fact rather than before it. Tax implications would need modeling. Liquidity adjustments would require recalibration. The portfolio's risk profile had shifted in ways the client had not fully considered, because he had not asked anyone to help him consider them.

David nodded and began asking clarifying questions. His voice remained professional. His attention remained steady. He would do the work. He always did the work.

The client had not intended disrespect.

He had simply acted first.

And in doing so, he had reduced David's role from counselor to coordinator—from someone whose judgment shaped the decision to someone whose expertise managed the aftermath. The revenue was the same either way. The relationship was intact. But the nature of the engagement had quietly shifted, and the compensation model had no way of recognizing that shift.

The next day, a different founder called with a different posture entirely.

"I haven't signed anything yet," he said. "I wanted to talk through this with you first."

They spent 90 minutes discussing timing, family governance, liquidity sequencing, and potential unintended consequences of accelerating a transaction. No spreadsheets were opened. No projections were displayed. They walked through implications instead—the kind of implications that only surface when two people are thinking together rather than reviewing apart. David asked questions the founder had not considered. The founder raised concerns David would not have anticipated. The conversation was not efficient. It was generative. And by the end of it, the founder had decided to slow the timeline by six months—a decision that would, in David's estimation, protect several million dollars in value that haste would have forfeited.

The structure rewarded both clients equally.

Revenue flowed from assets regardless of whether judgment had been invited early or late. The founder who called before signing and the client who called a month after committing capital both paid the same implicit fee. The firm's income statement could not tell them apart.

The difference was relational, not financial.

David began keeping a quiet ledger in his mind.

Received.

Tolerated.

The distinction was not moral. It was structural. He was not judging his clients. He was examining his practice—asking whether the way the firm earned its revenue reflected the way it actually created value.

Clients who received him did not simply appreciate performance; they invited discernment. They sought counsel before committing. They allowed space for disagreement. They treated advice as formative rather than confirmatory. They understood that what David offered was not information but sequence—the ability to know which decision came first, which conversation needed to happen before the document was signed, which family member needed to be in the room and which one did not.

Clients who tolerated him were not adversarial. They valued stability. They appreciated oversight. They were often grateful and kind. But they engaged him after momentum had already gathered, when the trajectory had been set and the room for counsel had narrowed. In those relationships, David was useful. He was not formative.

The compensation model did not differentiate between those postures.

It bundled them.

At the next partner meeting, recap modeling intensified. Updated valuation scenarios were distributed. Closing timelines tightened. Tax optimization windows were highlighted. The conversation had moved past whether to recap and was now focused on when and at what terms. The energy in the room was pragmatic and forward-leaning.

"If we don't move deliberately," one partner said, "we're leaving money on the table."

"We owe it to the team to secure infrastructure," another added.

No one framed recap as greed. No one spoke in terms of personal enrichment or competitive positioning. They framed it as prudence. As responsibility. As the natural next step for a firm that had earned the right to formalize what it had already built. And they were not wrong. David could see the logic as clearly as anyone in the room. He had made versions of this same argument to clients a hundred times.

The problem was not the argument. The problem was the timing. Once recap closed, the structure would be set. The firm's identity would be codified not just in operations but in obligations—obligations to a capital partner whose success was measured in growth rates and margin expansion. Those obligations were not unreasonable. But they were directional. And the direction they pointed was not the direction David's question was leading him.

Driving home that evening, David felt the earlier question sharpen into something closer to urgency.

If he stayed through recap, the structure would not drift toward alignment on its own. It would formalize. It would codify. It would embed growth expectations and compensation design more deeply into the firm's DNA. The assumptions he was questioning would become the architecture he was contractually committed to.

The option to revisit the question later would narrow.

It would not disappear entirely, but the cost of reconsideration would rise dramatically. He would not be reconsidering an informal structure. He would be unwinding a formalized one—with legal implications, financial consequences, and professional relationships at stake.

He parked in his driveway and remained seated in the car for a moment before turning off the engine. The dashboard lights dimmed and the silence settled around him—the particular silence of a car after the engine stops, when the world outside becomes audible again and the thoughts you've been outrunning catch up.

The house lights glowed softly through the windows. Nothing inside those walls demanded urgency. No crisis waited for him. Claire was probably reading. The dishwasher was probably running. The life they had built together was stable, warm, and sufficient.

That was what made the tension honest.

There was no external pressure forcing his hand.

Only an internal reckoning.

He had built a firm that worked.

He was no longer certain it reflected what he believed he was truly providing.

And once that awareness formed—once it had been named, examined, confirmed by a client fishing beside him in a river and echoed by a stranger in a ballroom—he knew it would not dissolve on its own.

Chapter 7

Benchmarks

The second meeting with the Chicago firm came in late May and it felt less exploratory and more procedural.

By then, the initial curiosity had matured into modeling. Financial projections were circulated in advance. Tax advisors had been consulted. Governance adjustments were mapped in draft form. What had begun as an option was steadily becoming a path—and paths, once established, develop their own momentum. Each step forward made the next step feel not only easier but inevitable.

The banker appeared on screen again, composed and precise, his tone unchanged from the first presentation. He spoke not of possibility this time, but of sequencing. The shift was subtle but unmistakable. The first meeting had been an invitation. This one was an itinerary.

"If you're aligned," he said, "we can move efficiently toward a year-end close. The market environment is supportive. Timing is favorable."

He walked through revenue expansion targets required to justify valuation. Recruiting acceleration. Productivity thresholds. Operational leverage ratios that would be measured quarterly once recap was formalized. Each metric was presented as reasonable—and each one was. Taken individually, no single target would have given David pause. It was the cumulative architecture that concerned him: the way each benchmark connected to the next, forming a system of expectations that, once accepted, would become the lens through which every decision at the firm was evaluated.

Nothing in the language suggested recklessness. It was disciplined. Institutional. The vocabulary of scale.

"We partner with firms that are already strong," he repeated. "Our role is to help you grow into your next phase."

David listened without visible reaction. He had spent much of his career helping clients evaluate similar transactions. He understood the appeal of institutional capital. He respected firms that scaled responsibly. He knew that recap, when structured well, was not predatory. It was strategic. He had counseled clients through comparable decisions and had sometimes advocated for exactly this kind of partnership—when the firm's identity and the capital partner's expectations were genuinely aligned.

That was the word that kept returning. Aligned.

But as the slides moved from valuation multiples to post-close expectations, something sharpened in him. Not objection. Recognition.

The model assumed acceleration.

Acceleration assumed production.

Production assumed growth as a defined objective.

There was nothing immoral in that sequence. It was simply explicit. And explicitness had a clarifying effect that ambiguity did not. As long as growth remained aspirational—something Northbridge pursued because it chose to—the firm retained the freedom to define success on its own terms. Once growth became contractual—something Northbridge pursued because it was obligated to—that freedom would narrow. Not disappear. Narrow. And David had learned, over 20 years of advising founders through transitions, that the difference between freedom and constraint often lived in exactly that narrowing.

After the banker signed off, the room remained quiet for several seconds. The kind of silence that follows a presentation so well-constructed that disagreement feels like a failure of sophistication.

"This is responsible," one partner said finally.

"It secures infrastructure," another added.

Michael leaned forward slightly. His posture carried the quiet authority of a man who had been preparing this argument for months and was now watching it land exactly as he had anticipated.

"We've reached a size where discipline demands structure," he said. "We can't operate informally forever."

The statement was not confrontational. It was factual. And it was, in its way, correct. Northbridge had crossed the billion-dollar threshold. Informal governance would not sustain indefinitely. Institutional capital provided guardrails and resources that private partnerships often struggled to maintain at scale. Michael was making the argument that any competent advisor would make to a client in the same position. David knew this because he had made it himself, many times, to many clients.

The difference was that he was no longer the advisor in this scenario. He was the client. And the client's perspective felt different from the inside than it looked from the outside.

David nodded slowly.

He did not challenge the logic.

He simply felt its weight.

Recap would not merely protect what they had built.

It would formalize what they were becoming.

And what they were becoming—a firm measured by growth velocity, margin expansion, and recruiting targets—was not what David believed the firm should be measured by. He did not think those metrics were wrong. He thought they were incomplete. They measured the firm as a business. They did not measure it as a practice. And the distinction between a business and a practice was, for David, not semantic. It was foundational. A business optimizes for growth. A practice optimizes for depth. Both can be excellent. But they are not the same thing, and a structure designed for one will, over time, quietly reshape the other.

Driving home that evening, he ran through the numbers again in his mind.

His personal liquidity distribution would be substantial. It would secure his family indefinitely. It would reduce risk in ways he had never fully experienced during the early years of building the firm, when every quarter felt provisional and every client departure felt personal. The money was real. The security was real. He would be foolish to dismiss it, and he did not dismiss it.

He imagined explaining the decision to Claire. The prudence. The discipline. The security. He could hear himself making the case, and he could hear how persuasive it would sound. Because it was persuasive. The argument for recap was not a bad argument. It was a good argument that happened to point in a direction David was no longer certain he wanted to go.

He also imagined quarterly board meetings where growth targets were no longer aspirational but required. Where margin expansion would be tracked against defined benchmarks. Where recruiting velocity would be measured against projections distributed to investors. Where the question in every room would shift, subtly but irreversibly, from "What serves this client best?" to "How does this fit within growth objectives?"

Perhaps that shift would be minor.

Perhaps he was overthinking it.

But he could not ignore the fact that recap would embed expectation into structure. And structure, he had taught younger advisors for years, shapes behavior more reliably than intention. He had said those words in training sessions and partner retreats. He had believed them when he said them. The question was whether he believed them enough to apply them here—to himself, to his own firm, at the moment when the cost of believing them was highest.

Later that night, after Claire had gone upstairs, he reopened the legal pad and studied the four columns again.

Recap no longer felt hypothetical.

It felt imminent.

He realized something else as he stared at the page. If he remained through recap, he would not easily revisit this question later. The transaction would anchor him financially and structurally. The liquidity he received would carry expectations. The governance he accepted would carry obligations. Leaving afterward would feel reactionary rather than deliberate—a man who took the money and then changed his mind, rather than a man who chose clarity before the money arrived.

The window was narrowing.

And narrowing windows demand clarity.

He closed the pad and turned off the light.

The numbers were strong.

The opportunity was real.

And the cost of inaction was beginning to look like a decision in itself.

Chapter 8

The Legal Pad

The house was quiet when David returned to the kitchen table that night in early June.

Claire had gone upstairs an hour earlier. The dishwasher hummed faintly in the background. A single lamp cast a soft circle of light across the wood surface where he had sat countless evenings reviewing client plans and firm projections. The rest of the kitchen receded into shadow, and the darkness beyond the windows reflected his own silhouette back at him—a man seated alone at a table, doing the work that no one else could do for him.

He unfolded the legal pad again.

The four columns remained where he had left them.

Recap. Optimize. Stay. Separate.

Earlier, the categories had felt theoretical—thought experiments arranged on paper to give structure to a restlessness he could not yet name. Now they felt personal. Each column represented not just a strategy but a version of the next decade of his life. A version of who he would be at sixty-five. A version of how his clients would experience him. A version of the story he would eventually tell himself about what he had done with the years he had left.

He began with Recap.

Liquidity. Stability. Infrastructure. Reduced personal risk. A stronger balance sheet. Institutional support for recruiting and expansion. The transaction would signal maturity. It would reinforce the firm's reputation in the market. It would make future succession more orderly. Every financial planner in the country would look at this column and nod. It was the textbook answer—the one David himself would have recommended to a client sitting in his chair, holding his pen, looking at his legal pad.

It would also anchor him.

Board oversight. Growth benchmarks. Defined expectations for margin expansion. Recruiting metrics. Productivity targets. A vocabulary of accountability that sounded responsible and was responsible—but that carried within it a quiet redefinition of what the firm existed to do. The firm would still serve clients. But it would serve them inside a structure optimized for growth, and growth would become the measure against which service was evaluated. Not the other way around.

None of those were inherently wrong. In fact, they were responsible. But they were explicit. And explicit expectations shape behavior whether anyone admits it or not. David had taught that principle for 20 years. He was staring at the proof of it now.

He moved to Optimize.

Northbridge could remain independent and refine internally. They could raise minimums. Increase revenue per household. Segment clients more aggressively. Tighten operating discipline without outside capital. It was the pragmatist's answer—change without disruption, improvement without upheaval.

It preserved autonomy.

It did not resolve the underlying question.

Optimize would refine the existing structure. It would not redesign it. It was the equivalent of rearranging the furniture in a house whose foundation you had begun to question. The rooms might feel different for a season. But the foundation would remain unchanged, and eventually the same discomfort would return—quieter perhaps, but no less real.

He stared at Stay.

Do nothing. Allow recap to proceed if the majority desired it. Maintain his equity position. Continue serving clients faithfully within the evolving structure. Revisit alignment later.

Later.

The word felt evasive now. It had the shape of responsibility but the substance of avoidance. David had heard clients use the word the same way—"We'll address the estate plan later." "We'll revisit the allocation later." "Later" was the word people used when they understood the question but were not yet willing to bear the cost of answering it.

Later meant after governance formalized. After capital anchored direction. After leaving would look like fracture rather than conviction.

Stay preserved reputation.

It did not preserve clarity.

He hesitated before writing beneath Separate.

The pen hovered above the paper for a moment—the kind of pause that is not about finding words but about accepting what the words will mean once they are written.

Sell equity independently. Leave before recap. Call clients one by one and explain something that would sound irrational to many of his peers. Risk being misunderstood. Risk being labeled restless or arrogant or ungrateful. Start again without inherited weather. Build a practice—not a business, a practice—from a foundation that reflected what he actually believed advisory work was for.

He thought about the employees who had built their careers under Northbridge's banner. Assistants. Paraplanners. Junior advisors who were still learning the craft and who relied on the firm's stability as the scaffolding for their own development. Would his departure destabilize them? Would it create uncertainty inside a firm that had prided itself on steadiness? He owed them consideration. He owed them a transition that did not prioritize his clarity at the expense of their security.

He thought about Rachel.

Ten years of shared work. Shared judgment. Shared trust with clients who had come to see the two of them as a unit. She had built her professional life around stability and discipline—the same values David admired in her, the same values that made her irreplaceable. Would he even allow her the option to follow? Or would offering that option place an unfair weight on a relationship that had always been characterized by mutual respect rather than obligation?

He had already decided one thing clearly.

He would not recruit.

If he left, he would leave cleanly. No whispered invitations in the hallway. No subtle positioning over coffee. No suggestion, however gentle, that loyalty required relocation. If anyone followed, it would be because they had arrived at their own question independently—not because David had planted it.

He thought about clients.

Some would follow reflexively out of loyalty. Some would stay reflexively out of caution. Some would hesitate, weighing the comfort of Northbridge's infrastructure against the depth of their relationship with David. Some would interpret his decision as ambition rather than conviction, and he would have no way to correct that interpretation without sounding defensive.

He forced himself to imagine a difficult conversation.

"Why would you leave at this point in your career?"

"Because I cannot reconcile the structure with what I believe I'm actually providing."

The answer sounded abstract even in his own mind. He could hear how it would land—vague to some, self-important to others, incomprehensible to anyone who measured success primarily in assets and revenue. And yet it was the truest thing he could say. He was not leaving because the firm had failed. He was leaving because the firm had succeeded at something he was no longer certain it should be optimizing for.

He wrote slowly beneath Separate:

Congruence.

He set the pen down and leaned back in his chair.

The truth was uncomfortable.

Recap preserved comfort now and direction later.

Stay preserved reputation.

Separate preserved congruence.

He was not choosing between right and wrong. No column was immoral. No column was negligent. Each one could be defended with intelligence and integrity. He was choosing between two different risks.

Risk of being misunderstood.

Or risk of being misaligned.

He sat in the quiet longer than he intended. The lamp hummed faintly. The refrigerator cycled off and the kitchen fell into a deeper silence—the kind of silence that feels almost physical, as though the room itself is holding its breath.

The numbers made sense.

The structure made sense.

The opportunity was real.

But obedience rarely announces itself through spreadsheets.

He heard her footsteps on the stairs before he saw her.

Claire appeared in the kitchen doorway wearing the reading glasses she only used late at night, a book held loosely at her side with one finger keeping the page. She did not look surprised to find him still at the table. She looked as though she had been listening to the silence beneath her and had decided it had gone on long enough.

"You're not coming up," she said. It was not a question.

"Not yet."

She set the book on the counter and pulled out the chair across from him. The legal pad sat between them, the four columns visible in the lamplight. She did not reach for it. She did not need to. Claire had a way of reading a room—its temperature, its weight—without requiring the document that caused it.

"Four options," she said, glancing at the pad.

"Four."

"And you've already eliminated two."

He looked at her. He had not said that to anyone. He had barely admitted it to himself. But she was right. Optimize and Stay had been dead since before he uncapped the pen. They were columns he had written to honor the process, not because they were real contenders. Claire had seen it the way she saw most things about him—not by studying the evidence but by studying the man holding it.

"How did you know?" he asked.

"Because you don't sit at this table past midnight for questions you've already answered," she said. "You sit here when you're afraid of the one you haven't."

The kitchen was still. The refrigerator had cycled off. The dishwasher had finished its run and gone quiet. The only light came from the single lamp above the table, and it cast their shadows long and steady against the far wall.

"What scares you about leaving?" she asked.

He had prepared for this question in the abstract—had turned it over during morning drives and quiet afternoons—but hearing it from Claire was different. She was not asking for analysis. She was asking for the thing beneath the analysis.

"That I'm wrong," he said.

"About what?"

"That I'm calling it conviction when it's really restlessness. That I'm dressing up ego in the language of alignment and walking away from something good because I've confused discomfort with calling."

Claire was quiet for a long moment. She removed her reading glasses and set them on the table beside the legal pad. The gesture was small, but David recognized it. She was shifting from listening to speaking. From receiving to offering.

"David," she said, "restless people don't agonize. They move. They find the next thing and chase it because staying still feels like dying. That is not what I'm watching."

She placed her hand flat on the table, near the legal pad but not touching it.

"What I'm watching is a man who has been sitting with the same question for weeks—not because he can't decide, but because he respects the cost of deciding. Restless people don't count the cost. You've counted it four different ways."

He felt the precision of that settle over him. It did not resolve the decision. But it answered the fear beneath it. If this were ego, it would have moved faster. If it were fatigue, it would have dissipated by now. What persisted was something quieter and more durable than either.

"What scares you about staying?" she asked.

The question landed harder than the first one. He opened his mouth, then closed it. The answer was forming slowly, the way answers do when they have been true for a long time but have never been spoken.

"That I'll spend the next decade knowing what I believe and choosing not to build from it," he said. "That I'll sit in quarterly meetings watching the structure move further from the work, and I'll be quiet, and I'll be comfortable, and I'll know."

Claire held his gaze without speaking. She did not rush to affirm or challenge. She simply held the space around what he had said, the way she had always held space for the things that mattered most—with stillness rather than solutions.

"Then you already know," she said quietly.

"Knowing and doing are different."

"They are," she agreed. "But the gap between them is where regret lives."

She stood, retrieved her book from the counter, and paused at the doorway.

"You don't need my permission," she said. "But you have it. You've always had it."

She went upstairs.

David sat alone at the table for a long time after that.

The legal pad remained open. The four columns were unchanged. The pen lay where he had set it down. Nothing in the room had moved. And yet everything felt different—the way a room feels different after someone has said something true in it.

He did not experience the decision as a moment of resolve. There was no surge of clarity, no sudden lifting of weight, no sense of having broken through a barrier. It arrived the way dawn arrives—not as a single event but as a gradual shift in what is visible. One moment the room is dark. The next, it is not. You cannot name the instant it changed.

But he knew.

He was not going to stay.

Not because staying was wrong. Not because his partners were misguided or the firm was failing. Not because recap was reckless or because institutional capital was inherently corrosive. He had spent weeks making sure none of those were the reasons, and he was satisfied that they were not. The firm would be fine. Better than fine. Michael would lead it well. The structure would serve many people faithfully for years.

It would simply not be his structure.

The realization carried no drama. It carried weight. The weight of knowing that what lay ahead would be harder, lonelier, and less certain than what he was leaving behind. The weight of knowing that some people would not understand. The weight of knowing that understanding was not required—only honesty.

He thought about Claire's words. The gap between knowing and doing is where regret lives. He had counseled clients through that gap for twenty years. He had watched men and women sit in his office with the answer already formed behind their eyes, waiting for permission to speak it aloud. He had been the voice that said: You already know. Trust what you know.

Now it was his turn to trust it.

He closed the legal pad. Not with resignation. Not with triumph. With the quiet finality of a man who has asked a question honestly and has received an answer he is willing to bear.

He turned off the lamp and walked upstairs.

The columns remained on the page.

But the question was no longer unresolved.

Chapter 9

Coffee Without Agenda

They met at a small coffee shop several blocks from David's office, not because it was private but because it was ordinary. The summer had arrived in earnest now—the sidewalk outside radiated heat even in the morning, and the large windows caught light that was sharper and more insistent than the filtered gray of the months before. The place was narrow, with dark wood tables and large windows facing the street. Morning light filtered through the glass, catching dust in the air and reflecting faintly against the polished floor. It was the kind of place where conversations blended together without anyone listening too closely. David had chosen it deliberately. What he needed was not secrecy but normalcy—a setting quiet enough to think in but common enough that thinking did not feel dramatic.

Harry was already seated when David arrived. He had a black ceramic mug in front of him and a folded newspaper resting beside it—the print edition, not a phone, which struck David as characteristic. Harry looked up as David approached and stood to shake his hand. His grip was firm and unhurried, the handshake of a man who had stopped being in a rush a long time ago.

"You look like a man who has done the math," Harry said after they sat down.

"I have," David replied.

"And it works," Harry continued, not as a question.

"Yes," David said. "It works."

Harry nodded slowly and took a measured sip of coffee. He did not rush to fill the silence. He had developed a habit, David had noticed, of allowing space to do its work before inserting language into it. It was a quality David recognized because he practiced it himself with clients—the discipline of not speaking simply to relieve discomfort. In Harry, the habit seemed less like technique and more like temperament. He was a man who trusted silence the way most people trusted words.

"Rational options are always available to successful men," Harry said at last. "That's part of what makes this difficult. If you were failing, the decision would be obvious. You'd have no choice but to change. But you're not failing. You're succeeding. And success gives you the luxury of staying exactly where you are."

David leaned back slightly in his chair. He had not realized how tightly he had been holding his posture until that moment—shoulders forward, hands clasped, the physical bearing of a man bracing for something he could not yet name.

"I don't want to become resentful," he said carefully. "If recap goes through and I stay, I don't want to sit in quarterly meetings feeling like I compromised something I knew needed clarity."

Harry watched him without interruption.

"I also don't want to create disruption that feels self-indulgent," David continued. "The firm is strong. My partners are disciplined. The transaction makes sense for them. I can see that clearly. I'm not questioning their judgment."

"You're questioning your own alignment," Harry said.

"Yes."

David hesitated before speaking again. He turned the coffee cup slowly in his hands, feeling the warmth of it against his palms.

"I'm not afraid of the numbers," he said. "I'm afraid of being wrong."

Harry tilted his head slightly.

"Wrong publicly?" he asked.

"Yes."

"And privately?"

David paused longer this time. The second question went deeper than the first. Being wrong publicly meant embarrassment, professional scrutiny, the quiet judgment of peers who would wonder what he was thinking. Being wrong privately meant something worse. It meant discovering, after the disruption and the cost and the uncertainty, that the question had been less profound than he believed—that he had mistaken restlessness for conviction.

"Yes," he said.

He stared at the table between them. The wood was scratched lightly from years of cups sliding across its surface. There was something grounding about its ordinariness—the small, accumulated evidence of a thousand conversations that had mattered to the people having them and to no one else.

"If I leave," David said slowly, "some people will assume ambition. Or ego. Or instability. They won't see alignment. They'll see disruption."

Harry did not contradict him and that was one of the things David valued most about their relationship. Harry did not offer false reassurance. He did not minimize the cost of difficult decisions in order to make them easier to reach. He let the cost stand and asked whether you were willing to bear it.

"And if I stay," David continued, "I may protect my reputation while losing congruence."

The word hung in the space between them.

Harry folded his hands and leaned forward slightly.

"You told me you believe your work is a calling," he said. "It is more than just compensation or accumulation. That what you provide to clients is not a service but a stewardship. If that's true—and I believe it is—then structure matters. The way you earn, the way you grow, the way you organize your attention—all of it either supports that calling or quietly erodes it."

"It does," David replied.

"Then this isn't about growth," Harry said gently. "It's about obedience."

David looked up at him.

The word was not dramatic in Harry's mouth. It was not heavy-handed or pious. It was almost quiet—spoken the way a doctor speaks a diagnosis that the patient has already suspected but not yet been willing to hear.

"I don't want to hurt my partners," David said.

"Then don't," Harry replied. "Leave cleanly. Without accusation. Without recruitment. Without positioning yourself as morally superior. If you go, go with integrity. Let the quality of your departure be the first evidence of what you're building."

David nodded slowly.

"I won't recruit," he said. "If I leave, I won't pull anyone with me."

Harry's expression softened slightly—not into approval, but into recognition. He understood what that commitment cost. In an industry where departure was often accompanied by a quiet campaign to bring clients and staff along, choosing to leave empty-handed was not just ethical. It was expensive.

"That matters," he said. "How you leave will shape what you build next. The foundation of the new thing is not the business plan. It's the character of the departure."

David felt the truth of that immediately. The temptation to justify departure by pointing to flaws in recap would be subtle but persistent. It would be easy to frame his decision as correction rather than conviction—to suggest, even by implication, that the partners who stayed were choosing comfort over principle. That framing would be dishonest. And it would poison everything he built afterward.

"I don't want to build the next thing by undermining the last one," David said quietly.

"Then don't," Harry replied. The repetition was not carelessness. It was emphasis. Harry had a way of saying simple things simply, trusting the listener to hear the weight behind them.

They sat in silence for a moment. The coffee shop had filled around them without either of them noticing. The espresso machine hissed. A barista called a name. Someone laughed at a table near the window.

"Tell me something," Harry said. "If you stay, what happens inside you?"

David did not answer quickly. He let the question sit, the way he would let a client's question sit when the honest answer required more than the immediate one.

"I quiet the question," he said eventually. "At least for a while. I tell myself that conditions will change, that alignment will come later, that the structure will evolve. And maybe it would. But I'd know, sitting in every meeting, that I had seen the question clearly and chosen not to answer it."

"And if you leave?"

"I expose it."

Harry nodded.

"Exposure feels like risk," he said. "But sometimes exposure is clarity. The things we are most afraid to reveal about ourselves are often the things that need to be built upon."

David looked out the window. A woman pushed a stroller past the café. A man in a suit crossed the street with hurried steps. The world moved forward, unaware of the internal negotiations taking place at their small table. And that was as it should be. The most important decisions, David had learned over 20 years of sitting with clients in their most consequential moments, almost never looked important from the outside.

"You're not choosing between right and wrong," Harry said finally. "You're choosing between comfort and congruence. Both carry cost. Only one preserves clarity."

David exhaled slowly.

"I thought courage would feel decisive," he admitted.

"It rarely does," Harry said. "It feels unsettled until the moment you act. And even then, it doesn't feel like courage. It feels like the only thing you could have done and still recognized yourself afterward."

The conversation drifted after that to smaller things. Family. Travel. The peculiar fatigue that comes not from work but from indecision—the way an unanswered question occupies more energy than a difficult one that has been resolved. Harry spoke briefly about his own departure from a firm years earlier, not in detail, but with enough honesty that David understood he was not receiving theory. He was receiving testimony.

When they stood to leave, Harry placed a hand briefly on David's shoulder.

"You already know," he said.

David did not argue.

As he walked back toward his office, the morning air cool against his face, he felt neither relief nor panic. He felt something quieter and more durable than either.

He felt alignment tightening toward decision.

The math still worked.

The opportunity was still real.

But the question had become clearer than the spreadsheet.

And clarity, he knew, demands response.

Chapter 10

The Line

David asked Michael for a private meeting late in the afternoon, after most of the staff had left for the day. He did not want the conversation overheard in passing or misinterpreted through half-closed doors. He had considered the timing carefully—not out of political calculation, but out of respect. What he was about to say deserved a room without an audience. Michael's office overlooked the western edge of the city, and by the time David stepped inside, the skyline had begun to shift toward evening light—that particular shade of amber that makes everything look both permanent and fragile at the same time.

Michael closed the door behind him and gestured toward the chairs across from his desk.

"I assumed we'd talk before the next partner meeting," he said.

David nodded.

"So did I."

There was no small talk. Both men had spent 20 years learning to read the weight of a conversation before a word was spoken. Michael knew this was not about a client review or a scheduling adjustment. David knew that Michael knew. The courtesy of pretending otherwise would have diminished them both.

"I'm leaving," David said.

Michael did not flinch. He did not ask what he meant. He did not repeat the word back in the form of a question. He had likely sensed the trajectory already—not from anything David had said, but from what David had stopped saying. The silences in partner meetings. The measured care with which he reviewed recap materials. The way a man's attention shifts when he is no longer building toward the same future as the people around him.

"Before recap?" Michael asked.

"Yes."

The word landed plainly. No qualification. No softening preamble. David had rehearsed this moment in his mind a dozen times—in the car, at the kitchen table, standing at the window of his office after everyone else had gone home—and each time he had resolved to say it simply. The moment deserved directness.

Michael leaned back in his chair and folded his hands. He did not look angry. He looked analytical—the way he looked when a client presented a decision that was emotionally clear but structurally complicated. It was, David realized, the same expression Michael wore when he was calculating consequences.

"You understand what this does to timing," he said.

"I do."

"And perception."

"Yes."

Silence stretched between them, not hostile but heavy. The kind of silence that exists between two men who have built something together and are now standing on different sides of a question neither one of them chose.

"Is this about the transaction?" Michael asked.

"No," David replied. "The transaction makes sense. I'm not opposing it. I'm not asking anyone to reconsider it. I believe it serves the firm."

"Then what is it?"

David chose his words carefully. Not because he was uncertain, but because he owed Michael precision. Vagueness here would be a form of disrespect.

"It's about alignment," he said. "I can't reconcile the structure we're formalizing with what I believe I'm actually providing. The model rewards accumulation. What I'm providing is judgment. Those aren't the same thing, and I can't formalize a structure that bundles them."

Michael studied him closely.

"That sounds abstract," he said.

"It's honest," David replied.

Michael stood and walked toward the window, hands in his pockets. The gesture was familiar. David had seen him do it a hundred times—when working through a valuation question, when considering a personnel decision, when absorbing news that required processing before response. He had built Northbridge with the same discipline David had. They had weathered downturns together. They had corrected missteps together. They had sat in rooms with angry clients and anxious employees and had never once turned on each other. This was not a shallow partnership. And that was precisely what made the conversation so difficult.

"You're walking away from meaningful liquidity," Michael said without turning around.

"I know."

"You're walking away at a moment when the firm is strongest."

"I know."

Michael turned back toward him. His expression had shifted—not to hostility, but to the particular gravity of a man trying to understand a decision that does not conform to his own framework for evaluating decisions.

"Then why now?"

David did not rush the answer. He owed Michael the same patience he would owe a client facing a consequential choice.

"Because if I stay through recap," he said slowly, "I won't revisit this question honestly later. The structure will be set. The incentives will be clear. Leaving afterward would feel reactionary rather than deliberate. I would be a man who took the money and then changed his mind. And that's not what this is."

Michael absorbed that. David could see him processing it—not dismissing it, but weighing it against his own understanding of what the firm needed and what David's departure would cost.

"You think we're misaligned," he said.

"No," David replied immediately. "I think we're disciplined. I think recap strengthens the firm. I'm not accusing anyone of anything. I'm not saying the partners who stay are making a mistake."

"Then you're making this about yourself."

"Yes," David said quietly. "I am."

The honesty shifted the air in the room. It was, paradoxically, the most selfless thing David could have said—because it refused to dress personal conviction in the language of institutional critique. He was not leaving because Northbridge was wrong. He was leaving because he needed to build something that was more precisely right for what he believed he was called to do.

Michael returned to his chair and sat down.

"And what about the team?" he asked. "The younger advisors? The employees who built stability here?"

David nodded.

"I've thought about them. Carefully."

"And?"

"I won't recruit," David said.

Michael's expression changed slightly—a softening that was almost imperceptible, but David saw it. It was the look of a man who had braced for something worse and found, instead, something he could respect.

"I won't solicit employees," David continued. His voice was steady. "No quiet conversations in the hallway. No positioning over lunch. No suggestion—however subtle—that loyalty requires relocation. If someone asks me directly, I'll answer honestly. But I will not initiate anything. The decision to follow, if anyone makes it, will be entirely their own."

Michael held his gaze for several seconds. The room was very quiet.

"You're entitled to speak to your clients," he said.

"I will," David replied. "They deserve clarity. They deserve to hear it from me directly, and they deserve to make their own choice without pressure. But I won't build the next firm by destabilizing this one."

The line felt firm inside him as he spoke it. Not rigid—firm. The difference mattered. Rigidity is brittle. Firmness is rooted. And what David felt as the words left his mouth was not defiance but foundation. This was the ground he would build on.

Michael exhaled slowly.

"That matters," he said at last.

"It matters to me," David replied.

There was no handshake yet. No resolution. The conversation had not concluded so much as it had arrived at a resting point—the place where two men who disagree can acknowledge the disagreement without destroying the relationship.

"You know this complicates recap," Michael said.

"I know."

"And you're prepared to carry that weight."

"Yes."

Michael leaned back again, his expression no longer analytical but reflective. Something behind his eyes had shifted—not toward agreement, but toward the kind of respect that only emerges when one person watches another make a costly decision without flinching.

"We built something good," he said.

"We did," David agreed. And he meant it completely. There was no bitterness in the words. No revisionism. Northbridge had been good. It had served clients well. It had provided for families. It had given David two decades of meaningful work and the financial foundation that now made this very choice possible. He would not dishonor that by pretending otherwise.

"And you're certain."

David hesitated only briefly. Not because the answer was uncertain, but because certainty, spoken aloud, becomes irreversible. Once he said yes, the architecture of the next chapter of his life would begin to take shape.

"Yes."

Michael extended his hand across the desk.

"I don't agree," he said. "But I respect that you drew a line."

David shook his hand. The grip was firm on both sides—the kind of handshake that carries weight because both men understand what it costs.

"That's all I'm asking."

When he stepped back into the hallway, the office felt the same as it had an hour earlier. Assistants were finishing tasks at their desks. The cleaning crew was beginning its rounds, moving quietly from room to room. The glass walls reflected muted evening light. Someone had left a jacket draped over a chair. A coffee cup sat abandoned beside a monitor.

Nothing had changed visibly.

Everything had changed structurally.

He had drawn the line.

Now he would have to stand inside it.

Chapter 11

The Room

The partner meeting was scheduled for late afternoon, when the day's client appointments had concluded and the office had quieted. The conference room looked exactly as it always had. The long rectangular table was polished. Water glasses sat evenly spaced at each seat. The skyline beyond the glass wall glowed faintly under a muted sky. It was a room designed for deliberation—for the careful, measured conversations that shaped the firm's direction quarter by quarter, year by year. David had sat in this room for nearly two decades. David had sat in this room for nearly two decades. He knew the grain of the table. He knew which chair creaked. He knew the way late afternoon light fell across the far wall and how it changed with the seasons—amber in summer, silver in winter, and today, in early July, something in between: warm but already starting to shorten. Nothing in the room suggested fracture.

Michael opened the meeting as he normally did, reviewing recap progress with disciplined clarity. Updated projections had been circulated. Legal counsel had refined language around governance adjustments. Tax advisors had confirmed closing advantages before year-end. The conversation moved with the practiced efficiency of people who had been building toward this moment for months.

"We're in the final stretch," Michael said. "Assuming alignment."

He did not look at David when he said it. Whether that was deliberate or incidental, David could not tell. But the word—alignment—landed differently in his ears than it would have a month ago. It had become a word with weight, a word that now divided the room in ways only two people in it understood.

Operational updates followed. Recruiting conversations. Margin refinement. A compliance question that was resolved quickly. The rhythm of a firm functioning normally—the ordinary machinery of a well-run practice doing what it had always done.

When the formal agenda concluded, David cleared his throat.

"I need a few minutes," he said.

The room settled. Not into silence, exactly, but into attention. The shift was subtle—a straightening of posture, a pen set down, a glass of water left untouched. They had all been in enough meetings to recognize the weight of a request that did not appear on the agenda.

He remained seated. He did not stand. He had considered standing and decided against it. Standing would have made this a performance. What he needed to deliver was not a speech but a statement. His hands rested lightly on the table in front of him.

"I won't be staying through recap," he said.

The sentence landed without volume but with force. It traveled across the table the way a stone drops into still water—a single point of impact, followed by rings that reach every edge.

Several partners froze in place. One leaned back slowly in his chair, as if creating physical distance from the words. Another looked immediately toward Michael, searching his face for a reaction that might help calibrate her own. Sarah Chen, the youngest partner nearest the door, lowered her pen without realizing she had stopped writing.

"You're leaving?" someone asked.

"Yes."

"For another firm?" another partner said quickly.

"No."

"Then what?"

David held the silence for a moment before answering. He did not use the silence for effect. He used it because the answer he was about to give had taken him weeks to arrive at, and he wanted to honor that process by not rushing its delivery.

"For something I would build today."

The phrase sounded different spoken aloud than it had in private reflection. In his own mind, it had carried the weight of conviction. In this room, surrounded by people who had built their careers and families around the firm's stability, it sounded like something else entirely. It sounded like departure.

"That's vague," one of the senior partners said flatly.

"It's honest," David replied.

Michael's expression remained controlled. He had heard this already. He had processed it, weighed it, disagreed with it, and respected it. But hearing it again in this room—watching it land on people who had not been prepared for it—was a different experience. David could see that.

"You're opposing recap," another partner said.

"No," David answered. "Recap makes sense. It strengthens infrastructure. It formalizes growth. I'm not arguing against it. I believe it serves the firm."

"Then why leave now?" Sarah asked. There was more confusion than accusation in her voice—the genuine bewilderment of someone who had admired David's leadership and could not reconcile that admiration with what she was hearing.

David chose his words carefully.

"Because I realized I wouldn't design the firm this way if I were starting in this environment," he said. "That doesn't make it wrong. It makes it misaligned—for me."

One partner leaned forward sharply.

"You're walking away from meaningful liquidity," he said. "That's not neutral."

"I know," David replied.

"Then what is it?"

He hesitated only briefly.

"Conviction."

The word hung in the room. It was the kind of word that either earns respect or invites skepticism, depending on whether the listener believes the person who says it. David could feel both responses forming around the table simultaneously.

A different partner spoke next, his tone measured but tight.

"You understand the message this sends to the market," he said. "We're in advanced conversations. Stability matters. A founding partner departing before close raises questions we shouldn't have to answer."

"I won't undermine recap," David replied. "I'll exit cleanly. No public criticism. No positioning. No obstruction."

"That's not the same as staying," the partner said.

"No," David agreed. "It isn't."

Silence returned.

The younger partner who had spoken earlier looked directly at him. Her expression had shifted from confusion to something more complex—something that contained both disappointment and, beneath it, the beginning of a question she had not yet asked herself.

"Why didn't you bring this up sooner?" she asked. "If you've been wrestling with alignment, why not discuss it before we reached this point?"

The question carried something more personal beneath it—perhaps disappointment, perhaps the particular hurt of someone who had trusted David's steadiness and now felt the ground shift beneath it.

"Clarity took longer than I expected," David said quietly. "I didn't want to introduce doubt until I was certain. I owed you certainty, not process."

"So we absorb the timing," she replied.

It was not an unfair statement. David felt the truth of it. His clarity had come at a cost to others, and he would not pretend otherwise.

"I know," he said. "And I'm sorry for the timing. Not for the decision. But for the burden it places on you."

Another partner shifted in his seat.

"You're not taking employees?" he asked.

David met his eyes.

"I'm not recruiting," he said. His voice was steady and clear. "I won't solicit anyone. No quiet conversations. No positioning. No suggestion that loyalty requires following me. If someone approaches me directly, I'll answer honestly. But I will not initiate."

The statement changed the tone of the room slightly. It did not resolve the tension, but it removed the sharpest edge of it. In an industry where departures were often accompanied by a campaign to bring staff and clients along—sometimes openly, sometimes through channels designed to look organic—David's commitment to leave empty-handed was unusual enough to register as significant.

"And clients?" the senior partner pressed.

"They will choose," David said. "I'll speak to each of them directly. They deserve to hear it from me. But I won't pressure anyone. I won't build the next thing by destabilizing this one."

"That sounds like recruitment," someone muttered from the far end of the table.

"It sounds like freedom," David replied calmly. "Clients are not assets. They are relationships. And relationships deserve the dignity of choice."

Michael finally spoke. He had been quiet throughout—not because he had nothing to say, but because he had already said it privately and understood that this moment belonged to the room, not to him.

"When?" he asked.

"Before year-end," David answered.

That tightened the atmosphere further. The recap timeline had already narrowed. His departure would alter perception whether he intended it to or not. A founding partner leaving before close would invite questions from the capital partner, from counsel, from anyone evaluating the firm's stability.

"You realize this complicates closing," the senior partner said.

"Yes."

"And you're prepared to carry that responsibility."

"Yes."

The room grew quiet again, but not the quiet of consensus. It was the quiet of recalibration—the sound of people adjusting their understanding of a firm they thought they knew, and of a partner they thought they had fully understood.

One partner shook his head slightly.

"I don't agree," he said. "But I respect that you're not attacking the firm."

David nodded.

"I'm not attacking it," he said. "We built something good. I'm grateful for every year of it. And I hope it continues to thrive."

He meant it. Every word. The room could hear that he meant it, and it mattered.

When the meeting adjourned, no one lingered to talk casually as they sometimes did. Papers were gathered more quickly than usual. Chairs slid back with sharper movements. Someone's phone vibrated against the table and was silenced with a quick hand. The ordinary sounds of departure carried an unfamiliar charge.

As David stepped into the hallway, the office felt altered in ways that were difficult to name. The same glass walls. The same muted lighting. The same names on frosted panels. But the air between those walls had changed. Conversations would shift. Interpretations would circulate. Some would defend him. Others would question him. Some would quietly wonder whether the question David had asked himself was one they should be asking too—and that wondering, more than anything else, was what made his departure significant.

He did not expect understanding.

He expected consequence.

And for the first time, he felt the full weight of having chosen clarity over comfort.

Claire was in the living room when he came through the door.

She was not reading. She was not watching the screen. She was sitting in the armchair near the window with a cup of tea held in both hands, the way she held things when she was waiting. Not waiting for him to arrive, waiting for whatever he would bring through the door with him.

He set his keys on the table by the entry and stood still for a moment. The drive home had been silent. He had not turned on the radio. He had not called anyone. He had driven through familiar streets with both hands on the wheel and his mind moving through the faces he had just left—the confusion, the disappointment, the controlled anger, the younger partner whose expression had shifted from admiration to something more complicated. Each face had stayed with him, imprinted by the gravity of what he had done.

"You told them," Claire said.

He had not called ahead. He had not texted. But she knew. She always knew. Not because she had any special access to the firm's internal life, but because she had spent twenty years reading the way David carried weight in his shoulders when a day had cost him something.

"Yes."

"Sit down."

He sat in the chair across from her. The living room was quiet in the way their house became quiet in the evenings, the deep, inhabited quiet of two people who had filled a home with children and noise and years and now lived inside the stillness that followed.

"How did it go?" she asked.

"About how I expected."

"That's not an answer."

He exhaled slowly.

"Some respected it. Some resented it. One of the younger partners..." He paused. "She asked why I didn't bring it up sooner. And she was right to ask."

"What did you say?"

"That clarity took longer than I expected."

Claire was quiet for a moment. She sipped her tea and set it on the side table with the careful, deliberate motion of a person who is choosing her next words with precision.

"Did anyone ask you what you were building?"

David thought about it.

"No," he said. "They asked what I was leaving. They asked about timing. About clients. About whether I was recruiting. No one asked what I was building."

"That tells you something," she said.

He looked at her.

"It tells you that the room was thinking about loss," she continued. "About what your leaving costs them. Which is natural. Which is fair. But no one in that room was curious about what you're moving toward. And that..." She paused, choosing the word. "That's the distance you've been feeling."

The observation landed with the quiet force of something he had known but not yet articulated. The partner meeting had felt adversarial not because his colleagues were hostile–they had been mostly measured, mostly fair, but because the entire conversation had been oriented around disruption. What does your departure cost? How does it affect the timeline? What signal does it send? Every question had been a form of damage assessment. Not one had been a form of inquiry.

"They're protecting what they built," he said. "I can't fault them for that."

"You shouldn't," Claire agreed. "But you also shouldn't confuse their reaction with your answer. Their questions are about their firm. Your question has always been about something else."

He leaned back in the chair and closed his eyes. The day had been long, far longer than the hours suggested. He felt the accumulated weight of weeks of private deliberation followed by minutes of public consequence. The decision was made. The words had been spoken. What remained now was the slow, unglamorous work of carrying it forward.

"Are you okay?" she asked.

"I don't regret it," he said.

"That's not what I asked."

He opened his eyes and looked at her. Claire was watching him with an expression he had seen only a handful of times in their marriage, not worry exactly, but something adjacent to it. The expression of a woman who trusted her husband's judgment completely and still needed to hear that the man behind the judgment was intact.

"I'm tired," he said. "And I'm sad. And I know those will pass."

She nodded slowly.

"The sadness means it mattered," she said. "If it didn't hurt to leave, it wouldn't have been worth building."

They sat together in the quiet for a long time after that. She did not offer strategy. She did not rehearse the next steps. She simply remained, present, unhurried, steady, the way she had always been present when the ground beneath him shifted. Not solving. Not softening. Just there.

When he finally went upstairs, the house held the stillness of a night that had changed something. Not dramatically. Not loudly. But permanently.

Chapter 12

Alignment

Rachel waited two days before coming to his office.

He had expected her sooner. She had been present in the partner meeting, seated near the far end of the table, listening without speaking as the decision landed in the room. She had not sought him out immediately afterward. She had not sent a text or left a note. She had returned to her desk and continued working through compliance documents as if nothing had shifted. David had watched her from across the office that afternoon and the next morning, looking for a signal—a glance, a hesitation, a change in her routine—and found none.

That restraint unsettled him more than anger would have.

When she finally entered his office, she closed the door behind her without knocking. The gesture was not rude. It was familiar. It carried the authority of a person who had earned the right to enter without ceremony— 10 years of shared work, shared decisions, shared silences after difficult client conversations. She remained standing for a moment, studying him as though she were confirming something she already suspected.

"You made a decision," she said.

"Yes."

"And you didn't ask me."

The words were not sharp, but they were direct. They carried the particular weight of someone who is not angry but disappointed—and who trusts the other person enough to say so without softening it.

"I wasn't going to recruit you," he replied.

"That wasn't the question," she said.

He felt the weight of that immediately. She was right. There was a difference between not recruiting and not including. He had been so committed to the ethical principle of non-recruitment—so careful to ensure that no one's decision was compromised by his influence—that he had failed to see the other side of it. By protecting Rachel from pressure, he had excluded her from partnership. And Rachel was not someone who needed protection from difficult questions. She was someone who deserved to be asked them.

"You didn't ask me," she repeated. The repetition was not for emphasis. It was for acknowledgment.

He stood from behind his desk and moved to the chair opposite her, sitting down so they were level rather than separated by furniture. The desk between them had always been a practical arrangement. Right now it would have felt like a barrier.

"I didn't want you to feel pressured," he said. "I didn't want my conviction to become your obligation."

Rachel crossed her arms, not defensively but deliberately—the way a person arranges their body when they are about to say something that has been forming for longer than the other person realizes.

"For 10 years," she said, "I've helped you execute decisions that weren't convenient. I've watched you tell clients hard truths when it cost revenue. I've watched you refuse incentives that would have made your life easier. I've reorganized compliance processes at midnight because you believed accuracy mattered more than sleep. And now you think I would default to comfort without even being included in the conversation?"

Her tone carried disappointment more than anger. It was the disappointment of someone who had been underestimated by the person she respected most.

"That wasn't my assumption," he said quietly.

"It feels like it."

Silence settled between them. The office hummed faintly around them—the ventilation, the distant sound of a phone ringing in the hallway, the muffled click of someone's keyboard. The ordinary sounds of a firm that was, for most of the people in it, proceeding normally.

"I made one decision clearly," he said. "If I leave, I won't recruit employees. No quiet conversations. No subtle positioning. I won't destabilize the firm to make my next step easier. That principle matters to me more than almost anything else in this process."

Rachel's posture softened slightly.

"I respect that," she said. "But not recruiting and not including are not the same thing."

He nodded. The distinction landed with the precision of a scalpel. She had identified the exact flaw in his reasoning without dismissing the reasoning itself. It was, he realized, exactly the kind of thing she had always done—the reason clients trusted her, the reason he trusted her, the reason she was irreplaceable.

She walked toward the window and looked out over the city before continuing. The late afternoon light caught her profile, and David was struck by how composed she looked—not calm in the way that conceals emotion, but composed in the way that reflects it clearly.

"You and I have built trust with clients together," she said. "You know that. They don't just trust you. They trust how we operate. How we sequence decisions. How we hold the line when something doesn't feel right. That's not your reputation alone. It's ours."

He said nothing. She was right, and anything he said would have diminished the truth of it.

"When recap conversations intensified," she continued, "I noticed the same things you did. Growth assumptions tightening. Production metrics becoming more explicit. The vocabulary shifting from 'what serves the client' to 'what meets the benchmark.' That's not immoral. But it's directional. And I noticed you noticing it."

She turned back toward him.

"I also know you," she said. "You don't leave because you're restless. You don't leave because you're bored or ambitious or chasing something shinier. You leave because you can't reconcile something internally. And when you can't reconcile, you don't pretend. That's why people trust you. And that's why I trust you."

The accuracy of it made him look down briefly. Being seen that clearly by someone who had worked beside him for a decade was both a gift and a weight.

"I didn't want to put you in a position where following me felt like loyalty instead of choice," he said.

Rachel sat down across from him. Her movement was deliberate—not the collapse of someone who is tired, but the settling of someone who has made a decision and is now prepared to declare it.

"I'm not coming out of loyalty," she said. "If I come, it will be because it aligns."

He met her eyes.

"And it does?" he asked.

"Yes."

The answer came without hesitation. Not because she hadn't considered it, but because she had been considering it—quietly, methodically, in the way she considered everything—since the moment David's words landed in the partner meeting two days earlier.

"I've watched you struggle with this quietly," she said. "I've watched you choose not to speak prematurely. I've watched you refuse to frame recap as wrong even when you knew you wouldn't stay. That tells me this isn't reaction. It's conviction. And I'd rather build something small and aligned than maintain something large and directional."

He exhaled slowly. The relief he felt was not the relief of having been joined—it was the relief of having been understood.

"It will be smaller," he said. "At least at first. Fewer resources. Less infrastructure. More exposure. We'll be building from the ground. Not from a platform."

Rachel nodded.

"And more clarity," she said.

He leaned back in his chair.

"You'll take heat," he said. "People will assume ambition or instability. They'll question whether this was really your decision or whether you were influenced."

"They may," she replied. "But the people who understand alignment will see it differently. And those are the only people I'm interested in building with."

Silence lingered again, this time steadier. The tension that had filled the first minutes of the conversation had resolved—not into agreement on every point, but into something more valuable: mutual clarity.

"When would you leave?" he asked.

"When you leave," she said. "I'm not staying to prove something."

He felt both gratitude and responsibility rise simultaneously. Gratitude because Rachel's presence would change everything about what was possible. Responsibility because her decision was now entrusted to his stewardship. If the new firm failed—if the economics were harsher than projected, if clients did not follow, if the market punished the departure—it would not be his failure alone. It would be hers too. And he would carry that weight as long as the work continued.

"I don't want you to regret it," he said.

"I won't," she replied. "Because I'm choosing it."

She paused before adding, more softly, "You didn't recruit me. You drew a line. I'm stepping across it on my own."

The distinction mattered. It was not a semantic one. It was foundational. The difference between being recruited and choosing to follow is the difference between obligation and conviction. And if the new firm was to be built on alignment, then every person who joined it needed to arrive by choice—fully, freely, and without the debt of having been persuaded.

They sat there for several minutes discussing logistics—timing, compliance requirements, communication sequencing, the practical architecture of two people extracting themselves from a firm they had helped build without leaving wreckage behind. The conversation was measured and specific, the way their conversations always were. But beneath the logistics ran something deeper: a shared understanding that what they were about to build would reflect not just strategy, but belief.

As she stood to leave, she turned back briefly.

"You did the right thing not to poach," she said. "If this next firm is built on alignment, it has to begin that way. The foundation can't be compromised by the method."

He nodded.

"I agree."

After she left, he remained seated for a long time. The office was quiet now. The light had shifted. The building was emptying as it did every evening, the ordinary rhythm of departure carrying on without interruption.

He had feared destabilizing others.

Instead, he had clarified who stood where.

Alignment, he realized, does not require persuasion.

It requires choice.

Chapter 13

The First Call

David closed his office door before dialing.

He had postponed this call longer than the others. A week had passed since the partner meeting and he had waited, not because he feared rejection, but because he respected the weight of it. Matt had been with him through more than portfolio reviews and quarterly updates. They had navigated succession planning together, working through the delicate architecture of transferring a business from one generation to the next without fracturing the family that held it. They had restructured family governance when relationships frayed under the pressure of shared wealth. And there was the late-night negotiation that nearly collapsed the sale of Matt's company years earlier—the conversation that had changed the nature of their relationship from professional to something closer to vocational.

Trust between them had been earned in tension, not convenience.

The phone rang twice before Matt answered.

"You're really doing this," Matt said without greeting.

"Yes," David replied.

There was no surprise in Matt's voice. News traveled quickly among clients who paid attention, and Matt paid attention to everything. He was the kind of man who notices shifts in tone before they become shifts in direction—who reads silences as fluently as he reads financial statements.

"Before recap closes?" Matt asked.

"Yes."

Silence settled between them. It was not the silence of disconnection. It was the silence of two men who had spent enough years in conversation to know that the space between words was where the real thinking happened.

David pictured him in his home office, likely seated at the same desk where they had reviewed sale documents years earlier—the desk where Matt had almost signed away leverage he would have regretted for the rest of his life.

"Why?" Matt asked finally.

The question carried more demand than curiosity. It was the question of a man who had invested not just money but belief in the person on the other end of the line, and who was now being asked to evaluate whether that belief still held.

David did not rush to answer.

"Because recap formalizes direction," he said carefully. "And I realized I wouldn't design that direction if I were starting in this environment. The structure rewards accumulation. What I provide—what I believe I'm called to provide—is judgment. And the model we're about to formalize doesn't distinguish between the two."

"That's abstract," Matt said.

David nodded, though Matt could not see him.

"Do you remember the night the buyers pushed that final concession?" he asked.

"I remember," Matt said immediately. The speed of the answer told David that the memory had not faded—that it lived in the same vivid, urgent register in Matt's mind as it did in his own.

"You were exhausted," David continued. "Your team wanted to sign. Legal said the language was minor—a governance provision that looked routine on paper. You were ready to close. You had been negotiating for months and the fatigue had accumulated to the point where any resolution felt better than continued uncertainty."

"I was done fighting," Matt said.

"And you asked me what I thought."

There was a pause. David could hear Matt breathing—the quiet, measured breathing of a man who is reliving a moment rather than simply recalling it.

"You said it wasn't minor," Matt replied.

"It wasn't," David said. "Not because of the numbers. Because of leverage. Because of what it would signal about governance going forward. Because conceding that language—at that hour, under that pressure—would have established a precedent that the buyers would have invoked again and again in the years that followed."

Matt exhaled quietly.

"That wasn't math," he said.

"No."

"It was judgment."

"Yes."

Silence returned, this time heavier. Both men understood what the memory meant in the context of this conversation. It was not nostalgia. It was evidence. David was not making an abstract argument about the nature of advisory work. He was pointing to a specific moment when the thing he provided—the thing that could not be replicated by software or scale or a 30-dollar-a-month planning tool—had protected Matt from a decision that would have cost him for years.

"If what you trust me for is judgment," David continued, "then the structure I operate within should make that explicit. I don't want it bundled quietly with market appreciation or growth assumptions. I want clarity. I want the way I earn to reflect the way I serve. And the structure I'm leaving doesn't do that. Not because it's corrupt. Because it wasn't designed for that."

Matt let the words sit. He did not respond immediately, and David did not fill the silence. They both understood that this was not a conversation to be rushed.

"You're not recruiting me," he said.

"No," David replied immediately. "You should evaluate what's best for you. Northbridge will continue to serve you well. The infrastructure is strong. The team is competent. I won't pressure you."

"You'd tell me if staying makes more sense?" Matt asked.

"Yes."

There was no hesitation in the answer. And Matt heard that. He heard the absence of salesmanship, the refusal to leverage the relationship for recruitment, the willingness to direct a trusted client toward a competitor if that was what served the client best. It was, in its way, the most persuasive thing David could have said—because it demonstrated the very quality he was claiming to build a firm around.

Matt was quiet for a long moment.

"You know how this looks," he said finally. "At your age. At this scale. Leaving when liquidity is on the table."

"I know," David replied.

"Ambition," Matt said.

"Some will see it that way."

"Ego."

"Possibly."

"Or restlessness."

"Maybe."

David did not defend himself. He did not attempt to reframe perception. He had learned—from years of sitting with clients in their most difficult moments—that defensiveness weakens a position more than silence does. If his decision was sound, it would become visible over time. If it was not, no amount of explanation would rescue it.

"Are you at peace?" Matt asked.

The question surprised him. Not because it was inappropriate, but because it came from a vocabulary that Matt rarely used in professional conversation. It was a personal question—the kind of question one man asks another when the relationship has moved past the transactional and into the territory of genuine care.

"I'm not comfortable," David said. "But I'm clear."

Matt laughed softly.

"That's not the same thing."

"No," David agreed. "It isn't. But I've spent 20 years telling clients that clarity matters more than comfort. If I don't believe that for myself, I have no right to say it to anyone else."

Silence again. The kind that carries respect.

"Send me what you're building," Matt said. "I'll review it."

It was not affirmation.

It was discernment.

Matt was doing exactly what David had always admired in him—refusing to make a consequential decision on the basis of emotion alone. He would examine the structure. He would evaluate the economics. He would weigh the proposition against his own needs and his family's interests. And then he would choose. Freely. The way every client deserved to choose.

David felt something tighten and release at the same time—the particular sensation of having spoken a truth and watching it land in a place where it would be taken seriously.

"I will," he said.

After the call ended, he remained seated, staring at the darkened phone screen in his hand. The office was quiet. The late afternoon light had softened to the point where the room felt more like a sanctuary than a workplace.

He had hoped for immediate loyalty. He had braced for immediate rejection.

He received neither.

Trust, he realized, does not eliminate evaluation.

It deepens it.

He opened the folder on his desk containing the draft outline of the new firm's structure. The pages were still rough—preliminary, incomplete, honest in their incompleteness. They described a practice, not a business. A structure built around judgment, not accumulation. A compensation model that made the source of value explicit rather than bundled.

He would send it.

And he would let Matt choose freely.

Chapter 14

Respectfully

The calls that followed were not dramatic.
They were human.

David scheduled them carefully, spacing them across several days rather than compressing them into a single afternoon. Each conversation required presence—not performance, but the kind of full attention that allows you to hear what a person is actually saying beneath what they are willing to say aloud. He did not want fatigue to shape tone or language. He did not want the tenth call to carry less care than the first. These were people who had trusted him with their futures. They deserved to hear this from a man who was fully present, not one who was managing a checklist.

Some responses were steady and uncomplicated.

One long-time client listened quietly as David explained the transition and the structure he was building. David described it plainly—what was changing, what it meant for the client, and what options were available. He did not dramatize the departure or minimize it. He offered facts and left room for questions.

"We're comfortable here," the client said at last. "The firm works for us. We know the team. We trust the process."

There was no criticism in his voice. Only preference. The client was not rejecting David. He was affirming a structure that had served him well and choosing to remain inside it. It was, David recognized, exactly the kind of rational decision he would have counseled a client to make.

"I understand," David replied. "You should remain where you're confident."

He meant it. He had told Harry he would not recruit. He had told Michael he would not pressure. Meaning it when a client chose to stay was the test of whether those commitments were principles or postures.

After hanging up, he sat still for several seconds. There was no anger. No defensiveness. But there was loss. Twenty years of shared work does not dissolve into neutrality simply because a structure changes. The client would remain at Northbridge and would be well served. David would move forward without him. And the relationship, built over years of trust and counsel, would gradually become a memory rather than a practice. That was the cost. He let himself feel it without rushing past it.

Another client surprised him in the opposite direction.

"We hired you," she said. "Not the logo."

Her tone carried warmth, almost defiance—as though she had already anticipated the conversation and had arrived at her answer before David finished his explanation.

David felt the temptation to accept that as validation. It would have been easy to let the affirmation fill the space that the previous call had emptied. But he had resolved to treat every conversation with the same honesty, regardless of whether the response was favorable.

"This will be smaller," he cautioned. "Less infrastructure at the beginning. Fewer layers of support. The transition will involve administrative disruption. I want you to understand what you're choosing."

"That doesn't concern me," she replied. "Clarity concerns me. I've watched you operate for years. I know what you're building toward, even if you haven't finished building it yet."

He thanked her and ended the call, aware that affirmation carries its own weight of responsibility. Every client who followed him was not just endorsing his conviction. They were entrusting their financial lives to a structure that did not yet exist. Their confidence was not a reward. It was a debt—one he would owe until the new firm proved itself worthy of it.

The harder conversations were neither affirming nor dismissive.

One founder, a man David had advised through two liquidity events and a family governance restructuring that had tested every relationship in his household, listened without interrupting. His silence was not passive. It was the silence of a man who takes things seriously and does not respond until he has fully absorbed what he has heard.

When David finished explaining, there was a long pause.

"I thought you'd see recap through," the man said finally. "It feels unfinished."

The word stayed with him.

Unfinished.

It was not an accusation. It was a feeling—the particular discomfort of watching someone you respect change course at a moment when you expected continuity. David understood it. He had felt it himself when clients made decisions he did not anticipate. The feeling was real even when the decision was sound.

"I understand why you'd feel that way," David replied. "Recap is not wrong. It strengthens the firm. I'm not leaving because it's flawed. I'm leaving because I can't reconcile it internally. And I would rather leave with honesty than stay with reservation."

There was another pause.

"I need to think," the client said.

"Take your time," David replied. "This is your decision, not mine. I'll answer any question you have, whenever you're ready to ask it."

After the call ended, David remained seated at his desk, staring at the legal pad where he had once drawn the four columns. The columns were still faintly visible, pressed into the paper beneath the page he had since written on. He had prepared himself for skepticism, but not for disappointment. Skepticism could be answered. Disappointment carried a quieter sting—the sting of realizing that your decision, however principled, has created a gap in someone else's experience of stability.

Then he called Thomas.

He had debated the timing of that call. Thomas was a man who valued deliberation the way some men value speed—as a discipline, not a default. He had recently sold his company after years of careful preparation, and the transition had required a recalibration of identity that David had witnessed firsthand. Thomas would not respond reflexively. He would listen, consider, and answer when he was ready—not before.

Thomas answered on the fourth ring.

"I heard," he said.

"Yes."

"You're leaving."

"Yes."

David explained the transition in measured language. He described the structure he was building—smaller, intentional, compensation aligned more directly with counsel rather than accumulation. He described it not as an improvement over Northbridge but as a different architecture designed for a different purpose. A practice, not a business. A firm built around the premise that what clients trusted him for—judgment—should be the thing the structure was designed to deliver and compensate.

Thomas listened without interruption.

When David finished, there was silence on the line. Not the silence of disconnection or disinterest, but the silence of a man who processes consequential information the way he processes everything else—slowly, carefully, and with an awareness that first reactions are rarely accurate ones.

"I just finished one transition," Thomas said at last. "Sold the company. Rebuilt my rhythm. Adjusted to a new normal. I'm not eager to move again."

David nodded, though Thomas could not see him.

"I understand."

"I'm not saying no," Thomas continued. "I'm saying not yet."

The distinction was subtle but significant.

Not yet meant uncertainty.

Not yet meant observation.

Not yet meant the burden of proof rested on David's alignment, not on Thomas's loyalty.

It was, David realized, the most respectful response anyone had given him. Thomas was not rejecting the vision. He was honoring it by refusing to endorse it prematurely. He would watch. He would evaluate. And if the new firm proved to be what David described—if the structure matched the conviction—then Thomas would consider it on its merits. Not before.

"I respect that," David said.

And he did. Completely.

After he ended the call, the office felt larger than before, the silence more pronounced. The early clients who had agreed to transition did not erase the weight of those who hesitated. Alignment did not guarantee momentum. Conviction did not generate pipeline. The math of starting over was not the math of compounding—it was the math of planting, and planting requires patience with bare soil.

He walked slowly down the hallway toward what would become the conference room of the new firm. The walnut table had not yet arrived. The room was still empty, echoing faintly with the sound of his footsteps on uncovered floor.

He stood there for several moments.

Leaving had felt clear in principle.

It felt thinner in practice.

For the first time since drawing the line with Michael, he felt the full cost of the decision—not as regret, but as weight. The weight of having chosen a path that required building rather than inheriting. The weight of knowing that every client who followed had placed a bet on his conviction. The weight of empty rooms that would need to be filled not by weather or momentum, but by the slow, deliberate work of proving that alignment was worth more than scale.

He had chosen congruence.

Now he would have to build without inherited weather.

Chapter 15

The Last Day

The final week at Northbridge came at the turn of August, when summer had reached the point where its abundance began to feel like weight.

There were no farewell lunches arranged by committee and no speeches drafted in advance. A short internal memo had been circulated after the partner meeting, written in restrained language that emphasized transition and continuity. Clients would be informed individually. Staff were instructed to direct operational questions to Michael. The memo said what it needed to say and nothing more. It had the tone of a document written by people who understood that the fewer words used, the fewer words could be misinterpreted.

The office functioned as it always had. Phones rang. Emails were answered. Client reviews proceeded on schedule. The machinery of a well-run firm continued to operate with the quiet precision that David himself had helped engineer over two decades.

That normalcy made the departure heavier.

On his last morning, David arrived earlier than usual. The parking garage was nearly empty. The elevator carried him upward alone. He moved slowly through the hallway before most of the lights were fully bright, pausing outside offices that bore the names of people he had once interviewed and hired. He had mentored several of the junior advisors when they were still unsure of their voice in client meetings—when they hesitated before making a recommendation, when they deferred to credentials rather than trusting their own observation. He had argued for promotions when the case was borderline, advocated for compensation adjustments when the numbers alone didn't capture what someone contributed, and absorbed more than one mistake without public correction because he believed that how a firm handled errors mattered more than whether it prevented them.

He stepped into his office and closed the door behind him.

The room looked the same as it had for years. Framed photographs on the shelf—Claire and the children at various ages, a group photo from a firm retreat that now felt like it belonged to a different era. A leather chair worn slightly along the edges, the leather darkened where his forearms had rested during thousands of conversations. A desk that had held thousands of client files, most of them no longer in paper form but preserved in memory nonetheless. He could have pointed to a spot on the surface and recalled the conversation that had taken place above it.

He packed deliberately, not hurriedly. A few books—ones that had shaped his thinking rather than decorating his shelves. A framed photograph of Claire and the children taken years earlier at a lake house, the light catching Claire's hair and the children squinting against the sun with the unselfconscious joy of people who do not yet know how quickly time moves. A small carved wooden box given to him by a client after a successful transition—the kind of gift that carries meaning disproportionate to its size, because the person who gave it understood what the work had cost.

The things he left behind were deliberate too. The firm's logo, etched into a glass award he had received at a conference. A bound copy of the original partnership agreement. A pen set given to the partners at the 10-year mark. These belonged to Northbridge. They should stay with it.

Mid-morning, a knock came at the door.

It was one of the younger advisors—the same one who had spoken in the partner meeting, whose expression had shifted from confusion to something more complex as David's words settled around the room.

"Do you have a minute?" she asked.

He gestured for her to come in.

She closed the door behind her and stood awkwardly near the chair across from his desk. She was holding a coffee she had clearly forgotten about—it had gone cold, and she held it more out of habit than purpose.

"I just wanted to say..." She hesitated. Not because she didn't know what she wanted to say, but because she was navigating the distance between professional composure and genuine feeling. "You were the first partner who let me lead a client meeting without stepping in."

He smiled faintly.

"You were ready."

"I wasn't sure," she said. "But you were."

There was no grand exchange. No emotional display. She thanked him and left. But as the door closed behind her, David felt something he had not anticipated—a specific, located grief. Not for the firm as an institution, but for the individual moments of investment that could not be transferred. The trust he had built with that young advisor, the patience he had extended, the judgment calls he had made about when to intervene and when to let her learn—all of that would continue to shape her career. But he would not be there to see it unfold. That was a cost he had not fully accounted for.

Shortly after lunch, a long-time client stopped by unexpectedly. He was not one of the clients David had called. He was staying with Northbridge. He had come simply to say something in person that he did not want to leave unsaid.

"I heard you were wrapping up," he said.

"Yes."

They shook hands firmly.

"You've always told me what I needed to hear, not what I wanted to hear," the client said. "That's rare. And I want you to know I noticed it every time."

David nodded. The words landed with more force than the client probably intended, because they confirmed the very thing David was building toward—a practice where that quality was not incidental but structural.

"Thank you," he said. "That means more than you know."

When the office began to quiet toward the end of the day—the gradual dimming of screens, the soft click of bags being gathered, the particular hush that falls over a professional space as it empties—Michael appeared at the doorway.

"Ready?" he asked.

David closed the last drawer and stood. He looked around the office once more. The walls were bare where photographs had hung. The desk was clean. The chair was pushed in. The room was already becoming someone else's.

They walked together down the hallway, past assistants who offered restrained nods—some warm, some uncertain, all aware that something had ended even if they could not fully articulate what it was. Past conference rooms where conversations continued as though nothing had shifted. Past the reception area where clients had first formed their impressions of Northbridge—the glass, the warm wood, the skyline visible but not imposing.

At the elevator, they paused.

"You built something meaningful here," Michael said.

"We did," David corrected gently.

Michael studied him for a moment. Whatever he saw in David's face—steadiness, perhaps, or the particular calm of a man who has made a decision and is no longer arguing with it—seemed to settle something in him as well.

"I still don't agree," he said. "But I understand that you're not leaving to attack what we built. And I respect the way you've handled this."

"I'm not," David replied. "Northbridge will do well. It deserves to."

Michael extended his hand.

"You're certain," he said. It was no longer a question. It was an acknowledgment.

"Yes."

They shook hands—not as adversaries but as men who had built something together and chosen different directions at its next stage. The handshake lasted a moment longer than protocol required, and neither man pulled away first. It carried 20 years of shared decisions, shared risks, shared mornings in this building when the work felt meaningful and the future felt open. All of that was in the grip.

The elevator doors opened with a soft mechanical hum.

As David stepped inside, he felt no surge of relief and no surge of fear.

He felt gravity.

The weight of what he was leaving and the weight of what he was walking toward, held together in the same body, carried by the same conviction, moving in the same direction.

The doors closed.

He descended without looking back.

Chapter 16

Proportion

The first office space David toured was practical.

It occupied a shared executive suite on the third floor of a mid-rise building that housed attorneys and consultants. The lease terms were flexible. The overhead was low. The furnishings were neutral and efficient—the kind of furniture that belongs to no one in particular, chosen not for what it communicates but for what it doesn't cost. It would allow him to operate quietly while testing assumptions about the new firm.

The real estate broker described it as "a prudent first step."

David walked through the space slowly, running his hand across a laminate conference table that had likely hosted dozens of small professional startups—businesses that began here and either outgrew the space or folded without leaving a mark on it. The walls were painted in a neutral gray that attempted seriousness without personality. The ceiling tiles were standard commercial grid. The carpet showed the faint, generalized wear of years of interchangeable tenants.

It would function.

He thanked the broker and declined.

He was not testing. He had spent months testing—testing the question, testing the conviction, testing the strength of his own clarity against the reasonable objections of people he respected. The testing was over. What he needed now was not a provisional space. He needed a space that reflected, from the first day, what the firm was designed to be.

The second option sat at the opposite extreme.

A corner suite in a newly renovated building near the financial district. Floor-to-ceiling glass. Premium signage rights. Architectural lighting designed to create presence from the street below. The broker spoke about visibility and brand reinforcement. He used phrases like "first impression" and "market positioning" and "signaling credibility." The language was not wrong. It was simply designed for a different kind of firm.

David stood near the window and imagined clients stepping into the space.

It was impressive.

It was also performative.

He had liquidity now. The independent sale of his equity position had provided more than sufficient capital to secure something like this without strain. He could afford the premium signage and the architectural lighting and the corner suite that announced success to anyone walking past on the sidewalk below. He could afford it easily.

That was precisely why he hesitated.

He had watched clients make this mistake before—the mistake of allowing capacity to dictate scale. Because you can afford it, you assume you should have it. Because the money is available, you let it define the size of the decision. David had counseled founders against this instinct for 20 years. He had sat across from men and women who had just received meaningful liquidity and helped them understand that the most dangerous moment in financial life is not scarcity. It is abundance. Scarcity forces discipline. Abundance permits indulgence. And indulgence, left unchecked, quietly replaces intention.

He was not trying to signal ascent.

He was trying to embody alignment.

He declined that space as well.

The third building sat slightly back from the road in a quieter part of the business district. Mature trees framed the entrance—oaks, old enough that their canopy shaded the sidewalk in summer, and their bare branches gave the building a kind of structural honesty in winter. The exterior was stone and glass, understated without being dated. The lobby was well-maintained but not theatrical. There was natural light, but not spectacle. A person entering this building would not feel intimidated. They would feel received.

The suite itself was empty when he entered.

High ceilings. Solid wood trim. Windows that faced east, catching morning light rather than afternoon glare. The layout allowed for a conference room with presence but without hierarchy—a room where the table, not the décor, would be the center of attention. Where conversations would feel important because of what was being discussed, not because of what surrounded the discussion.

He walked the perimeter twice before speaking.

"This is available immediately?" he asked.

"Yes," the broker replied.

He stepped into what would become the conference room and stood alone for a moment. The empty room held the particular silence of a space that is waiting to be defined—not empty in the way of abandonment, but empty in the way of potential. He could feel the conversations that would take place here. Not yet. But soon.

He was not constrained by capital. He could have chosen larger. He could have chosen smaller. He could have operated remotely and saved overhead entirely.

The question was not cost.

It was proportion.

What size reflected the firm he intended to build? Not aspirationally—not the firm he hoped it might become in five years or 10—but honestly. The firm as it was right now. Two people. A handful of transitioning clients. A conviction that had not yet been tested by a single quarter of operation. The space needed to reflect that reality without apology and without pretension.

He signed the lease that afternoon.

When he transferred the deposit, there was no anxiety attached to the number. Years of disciplined accumulation had removed fear from the equation. He was not risking security. He was allocating it. The distinction mattered. Risk implies uncertainty about outcome. Allocation implies intention about deployment. David knew precisely what he was doing and why he was doing it. The money was not leaving his control. It was being directed toward something he believed in—and belief, when it is genuine, does not feel like risk. It feels like alignment.

Over the following weeks, he worked with an architect not to impress but to align. The reception area would be simple but intentional—a place where a client would feel welcomed rather than evaluated. The materials would be durable, not decorative. The lighting would be warm, not dramatic. He chose local art from a gallery owned by a client who had once described his own work as "craft, not production." The phrase had stayed with David. It described what he was building.

He selected a rug woven by a small regional workshop rather than ordering from a commercial supplier—not because it was more expensive, but because it was specific. It had been made by particular hands in a particular place, and it carried the character of that specificity in a way that a factory product could not. He purchased chairs that would age well, built from hardwood rather than composite. Chairs that would darken and soften over years of use, becoming more themselves with time rather than less.

None of it was extravagant.

None of it was careless.

Each decision carried the same internal question: Does this reflect what we believe we are building?

When Rachel walked through the nearly finished space for the first time, she paused near the entry. She stood still for several seconds, taking it in without commentary—the way she took in everything, processing it fully before offering a response.

"It feels intentional," she said.

"That was the goal," he replied.

"You could have gone bigger."

"Yes."

"You could have gone leaner."

"Yes."

She nodded.

"This feels proportionate."

He agreed. The word was exactly right. Not impressive. Not modest. Proportionate. It was the spatial equivalent of what he was trying to build in every other dimension of the firm—a structure where the size of the thing matched the substance of it. Where nothing was inflated and nothing was diminished. Where a client could walk in and feel, without being told, that the people inside this space took their work seriously and did not need the space to prove it.

The capital he had earned gave him freedom.

But freedom untethered from alignment is merely indulgence.

He did not want indulgence.

He wanted clarity embodied in walls and wood and light.

The conference room remained empty for several weeks after the rest of the furniture was installed. The chairs were there. The credenza was there. The art was hung. But the center of the room held only open floor.

He had not yet ordered the table.

Claire came to see the space on a Saturday morning.

He had not asked her to. She had said, over coffee, that she wanted to see it, not the renderings or the floor plans he had spread across the kitchen table in recent weeks, but the actual room. The physical thing. She wanted to stand inside it.

They drove together through weekend streets that were quieter than their weekday versions, the same intersections, the same buildings, but emptied of the urgency that normally filled them. David parked in front of the building, and they walked in through the lobby without speaking. The elevator was small and unhurried. The hallway on their floor smelled faintly of fresh paint and new carpet.

He unlocked the door and stepped aside to let her enter first.

Claire moved through the space slowly. She touched the trim around the doorframe. She paused in the reception area and looked at the artwork, the piece from the gallery client, hung where visitors would see it first. She ran her hand along the edge of the credenza in the hallway the way a person runs their hand along something they are trying to understand through texture rather than sight.

She did not narrate. She did not evaluate. She simply moved through each room with the quiet attention of someone who understood that this space was not furniture and square footage. It was a declaration.

When she reached the conference room, she stopped.

The room was empty. The chairs were arranged along the perimeter. The art was hung. But the center of the room held only open floor, the space where the table would go, once David decided what the table should be.

Claire walked to the center and stood there.

"This is where it happens," she said.

"Yes."

"The conversations."

"All of them."

She turned in a slow circle, taking in the windows, the light, the proportion of the room. Then she looked at him with an expression that carried more than approval. It carried recognition.

"You're different," she said.

"How?"

She considered the question the way she considered most things, without rushing, without performing certainty.

"Quieter," she said. "But not smaller. You used to carry the firm's noise with you everywhere. In the car. At dinner. In bed at night, staring at the ceiling, running numbers. You carried it like it was yours to hold."

He listened without interrupting.

"Now there's less noise," she continued. "But more weight. The good kind. The kind that comes from choosing something deliberately instead of inheriting it."

David felt the truth of that settle into the empty room around them. He had noticed it himself, a shift in the quality of his attention. At Northbridge, his mind had been full of operational rhythm: recruiting metrics, margin targets, the steady hum of a machine that ran whether he was present. Now his mind was full of something else entirely. Not less. Different. The weight of building from nothing, of having no inherited momentum, of knowing that every client who came through this door would come because of a relationship, not a structure.

"Are you worried?" he asked.

She looked at him directly.

"I was worried at the kitchen table," she said. "When you were sitting with the question and I didn't know if you'd trust yourself to answer it. I'm not worried now."

"Why not?"

"Because this room looks like you," she said. "Not the version of you that managed a firm. The version of you that sat across from Matt on a river and knew exactly what kind of advice mattered. That's who built this room."

She walked to the window and looked out at the trees that framed the building's entrance—the oaks that David had noticed on his first visit, the ones whose canopy would shade the sidewalk in summer.

"You need a table," she said.

"I know."

"Not from a catalog."

He smiled. It was the first time in weeks that something had landed lightly enough to produce a smile, and it came from the person who knew him well enough to say in six words what had taken him days to articulate to himself.

"No," he said. "Not from a catalog."

They stood together in the empty conference room for another moment—the morning light catching the floor, the trees moving gently outside the window, the room holding its silence like a promise. Then Claire turned and walked back toward the door.

"Build it right," she said without turning around.

He intended to.

Chapter 17

The Table

David stood in the empty conference room longer than he intended.

The rest of the office had taken shape. The reception area was finished—simple, warm, the kind of space where a client would feel welcomed rather than evaluated. The artwork had been installed. The lighting had been adjusted until it felt warm without being dim. Even the smaller details—the placement of books on shelves, the arrangement of chairs in the waiting area, the weight and texture of the paper used for the firm's first stationery—had been considered carefully. Each choice had passed through the same filter: Does this reflect what we believe we are building?

But the conference room remained incomplete.

There was space in the center where the table would sit, and without it the room felt suspended, as if waiting for its anchor. The chairs were arranged in a loose arc along the perimeter. The credenza held nothing yet. The art on the walls seemed to lean inward slightly, as though converging toward a center that had not yet been defined.

He could have ordered from a national manufacturer. A polished catalog would have provided dozens of options—cherry, maple, glass, composite—in every dimension and finish. Delivery could be arranged within weeks. The process would be simple and efficient. It was what most firms did, and it produced perfectly adequate results.

Instead, he dialed Thomas.

The phone rang longer than usual before Thomas answered.

"This isn't about accounts," David said as soon as Thomas greeted him.

"I figured," Thomas replied. There was a note of dry amusement in his voice—the tone of a man who has learned to read the opening line of a conversation the way a fisherman reads the surface of water.

"I'm furnishing the office," David continued. "And I want you to build the conference table."

There was a pause long enough to register surprise. Thomas had sold his company, but the workshop had remained. It was part of who he was—the physical expression of a man who had built a business with his hands and who still found clarity in the act of making something tangible from raw material.

"You're serious," Thomas said.

"Yes."

"Even though I haven't moved my accounts."

"Yes."

The workshop noise seemed to quiet for a moment, as if Thomas had stepped away from the machines. David could picture him standing near the open bay door, phone pressed to his ear, sawdust settling faintly on his shoulders.

"Why?" he asked.

David did not rush the answer. He owed Thomas the same deliberation Thomas had shown him.

"Because I would rather build this place with people I trust," he said, "than order it from a catalog. The table is going to be the center of the practice. It's where every important conversation will happen. I want it built by someone who understands what those conversations cost."

Silence.

"I told you I wasn't ready to move," Thomas said.

"I know."

"And you're still calling."

"Yes. I'm not asking you to move your accounts. I'm asking you to build a table. Those are different things."

Another pause. David could almost hear Thomas processing the distinction—recognizing that David was honoring his "not yet" while still including him in the building. It was the inverse of what David had done with Rachel, and he had learned from that mistake. Not including was its own form of exclusion. This time, he was offering participation without requiring commitment.

"What are you thinking?" Thomas asked at last.

"Walnut," David said. "Solid. Round. No head."

"No head?" Thomas repeated.

"No dominant position," David replied. "Everyone seated equally. No one at the head of the table because there is no head. The shape itself communicates the posture."

Thomas let out a faint breath that might have been a laugh—or might have been recognition.

"You've thought about this."

"Yes."

"Size?"

"Large enough to hold difficult conversations," David said. "Small enough that no one disappears."

Thomas was quiet again. When he spoke, his voice had shifted—not toward agreement about accounts, but toward the particular engagement of a craftsman who has been asked to build something meaningful.

"This isn't temporary, is it?" he asked.

"No."

"All right," Thomas said finally. "I'll come measure."

When Thomas arrived the following week, he walked through the office slowly. He did not comment on the business. He did not ask about clients or revenue or operational plans. He was there as a builder, and he moved through the space the way a builder moves—with his hands as much as his eyes, touching surfaces, testing weight, reading the room the way he would read a piece of wood before cutting it.

He studied the light coming through the eastern windows in the morning. He ran his hand along the trim. He stood in the center of the conference room and looked upward at the ceiling height, then down at the floor, then across to the windows, measuring proportions that only a person who builds things by hand instinctively calculates.

"You didn't go small," he observed.

"No."

"You didn't go flashy either."

"That wasn't the goal."

Thomas nodded. The nod carried approval—not of the business decision, which he had not yet endorsed, but of the aesthetic one. The space was proportionate. It reflected intention without performing it. He could respect that, even from a position of observation.

They spoke about wood selection and grain direction. About how walnut deepens in tone over time, moving from a lighter brown toward something richer and more complex as years of light and air and the oils from human hands gradually transform the surface. About how a round table requires careful joinery to maintain structural integrity without visible seams—how the wood must be selected not just for appearance but for how it will move and settle over decades.

"There's no hiding flaws in a round table," Thomas said. "Rectangular tables have edges and corners that break the eye. A round surface is continuous. Everything is exposed."

"That's appropriate," David replied.

The line hung in the air between them. Both men understood that David was not talking only about furniture.

The table arrived six weeks later.

It took four men to carry it up the stairs and through the doorway, angling it carefully around corners that seemed designed for smaller things. The wood was darker than David expected—Thomas had selected boards from the heartwood, where the grain was tightest and the color deepest. The surface flowed in subtle arcs, the grain moving in patterns that were visible but not uniform, the way natural things move when they have not been forced into symmetry.

When the table was set down in the center of the room, the space it occupied shifted immediately. The room that had felt provisional for weeks suddenly had a center of gravity. The chairs, the credenza, the art on the walls—all of it now organized itself around the table, as though the room had been designed for this specific object and had simply been waiting for it to arrive.

It no longer felt provisional.

David ran his hand lightly across the surface. The wood was smooth but not slick—finished in a way that preserved the texture of the grain beneath the seal. It invited touch. It would warm under a hand. It would hold the weight of documents and coffee cups and elbows and the heavy silences that accompany the most important decisions a family can make.

It was not ostentatious.

It was substantial.

Rachel stood in the doorway for several minutes before speaking. She had the expression of someone encountering something that confirms what they had hoped but had not yet seen—the physical proof that the thing they were building was real.

"You bought this after he said not yet," she said.

"Yes."

"You didn't wait for him to follow."

"No."

She stepped closer and placed her hand on the wood. Her fingers rested there for a moment, feeling the grain, the warmth, the solidity of it.

"That matters," she said.

He understood what she meant. The table was not leverage. It was not a gesture designed to influence Thomas's decision about moving his accounts. It was alignment—the physical expression of a commitment that did not depend on someone else's response. David had asked Thomas to build it not because Thomas was a client, but because Thomas was a craftsman. And the table would stand in the center of the practice whether Thomas ever moved his accounts or not. Its value was intrinsic, not conditional.

That afternoon, he sat alone in the room and imagined the first client conversation that would take place there. Not as performance, but as practice. Difficult decisions made without hierarchy. Discernment invited without pressure. A founder asking whether to sell. A family navigating the silence that follows a death. A couple realizing that their assumptions about retirement no longer held. The table would hold all of it.

Thomas had not followed yet.

But the table sat firmly in place.

And for the first time since leaving Northbridge, the rebuild felt less theoretical and more embodied. The conviction that had carried David through months of deliberation and departure now had a surface. It had grain and weight and warmth. It occupied space in the world.

Alignment had become physical.

Chapter 18

Drift

The first 90 days did not feel dramatic.

They felt deliberate.

Fourteen client households transitioned in the first wave. The custodial accounts moved without complication. Planning software was configured. Reporting systems were tested and retested until Rachel was satisfied that nothing would fall through during the first quarter of live operation. The compliance calendar was rebuilt from the ground up—not imported from Northbridge, but designed from scratch, because David believed that even administrative architecture should reflect the firm's values rather than inherit someone else's. Rachel moved through operational details with the same steady precision she had always brought to Northbridge. Her presence made the transition feel less like a startup and more like a continuation—as though the quality of the work had simply relocated.

On paper, the firm was stable.

Revenue projections aligned with expectations. Expenses were proportionate to scale. Liquidity from David's equity sale meant there was no immediate financial pressure. There was margin—enough to operate without urgency, enough to make decisions based on conviction rather than cash flow. By every measure David had established in his own projections, the firm was performing exactly as planned.

But there was also quiet.

At Northbridge, growth had often arrived unannounced. A client would mention a colleague at dinner and a phone call would follow. A CPA would introduce a business owner in passing and within weeks a new relationship had formed. Market appreciation would expand revenue without any new meeting being scheduled. Recruiting conversations would generate additional assets organically. The firm had existed inside a system of compounding momentum—each year building on the accumulated gravity of the years before it.

Here, there was no weather.

The calendar reflected only what had been intentionally placed there. Every meeting was the result of a specific invitation. Every conversation was the product of a deliberate relationship. Nothing arrived on its own. Nothing compounded in the background while David attended to other things. The silence between scheduled appointments was not peaceful. It was conspicuous.

One evening, after Rachel left for the day, David remained seated at the walnut table reviewing the quarter's numbers. The overhead lights were dimmed slightly, and the room carried the faint scent of wood and paper. Outside the eastern windows, the sky had darkened, and his reflection stared back at him from the glass—a man alone at a round table, surrounded by chairs that were not yet occupied by the conversations they had been chosen to hold.

The numbers worked.

They did not expand.

He stared at the revenue column longer than necessary. It was sufficient. Sustainable. Honest. It reflected exactly what 14 households of intentional, judgment-based advisory work produced. There was no inflation in it. No market appreciation masquerading as earned revenue. No weather filling the gaps between engagements.

It was not accelerating.

He leaned back in his chair and let the thought form without resisting it.

What if alignment costs velocity?

He did not feel panic. He felt exposure. The particular exposure of a man who has removed every structural buffer between himself and the truth of his own production. At Northbridge, the model had obscured the distinction between revenue earned and revenue that arrived. Here, there was nowhere to hide. Every dollar of income was directly attributable to a relationship David or Rachel had built, a conversation they had initiated, a client who had chosen to be there. The clarity he had sought was now complete—and complete clarity, he discovered, is not always comfortable.

He had chosen to leave a billion-dollar firm where momentum was structural. Here, momentum would have to be cultivated deliberately. Every introduction would require intention. Every conversation would require invitation. Every new client would arrive not because the firm's size attracted them, but because the firm's character did. And character, unlike scale, does not compound automatically.

He traced the grain of the walnut table with his fingertips. The wood was warm under his hand. Thomas had built this surface to last decades. But a table does not fill a room with conversation. It only provides the surface for it.

Had he mistaken clarity for growth?

Had he assumed that alignment would produce gravity quickly—that doing the right thing, structurally and ethically, would generate its own momentum?

He thought of the clients who had hesitated. Of Thomas's "not yet." Of Matt's measured evaluation. Of the founder who had said "unfinished" with a disappointment David could still feel. These were not rejections. They were deferrals. But deferrals do not generate revenue. They generate patience. And patience, in the early months of a new firm, feels indistinguishable from drift.

He had told himself he was not leaving for expansion.

But somewhere beneath that conviction—beneath the careful language about alignment and congruence and building where you are received—he had assumed momentum would follow integrity. He had believed, without fully admitting it, that the rightness of the decision would produce its own results. That conviction would attract. That clarity would compound.

Now he was not so sure.

The following morning, he called Michael and asked to meet for coffee.

They chose a neutral location midway between the old office and the new—a place that belonged to neither of them, where the conversation could exist outside the gravitational field of either firm.

Recap had closed successfully. Northbridge had announced the transaction publicly. Recruiting efforts had intensified. Press coverage had circulated within the industry. From the outside, Northbridge looked exactly as institutional capital intended it to look—larger, more stable, more formalized. Michael had executed the transition with the same discipline he brought to everything.

"How's it going?" Michael asked.

"It's stable," David replied.

Michael nodded.

"And?"

"It's thin."

The word cost him something to say. Not because it was untrue, but because saying it to Michael—the person who had warned him, who had disagreed with his decision, who had shaken his hand at the elevator with the steady grip of a man who expected to be proven right—required a kind of honesty that went beyond professional courtesy.

Michael smiled faintly, not unkindly. There was no satisfaction in his expression. Whatever David expected—vindication, perhaps, or a subtle I-told-you-so—he did not find it. What he found instead was the quiet recognition of one builder acknowledging another builder's difficulty.

"Predictability has value," he said.

"Yes," David replied.

"You left that."

"I know."

Michael stirred his coffee slowly.

"You were never afraid of building," he said. "But you were accustomed to scale. And scale has a gravity that you don't notice until it's gone. It pulls things toward you—clients, referrals, opportunities—not because you earned each one individually, but because the structure itself attracted them. When you remove that structure, you remove that pull. What's left is only what you can generate yourself."

David did not argue. Michael was right. And the fact that Michael could say it without malice—could diagnose the difficulty without weaponizing it—told David something important about the man he had partnered with for 20 years. Michael disagreed with the decision. He did not resent the person who made it.

"I didn't leave for predictability," David said.

"No," Michael agreed. "You left for conviction."

They sat in silence for a moment. The coffee shop hummed around them. Two men who had built something together, sitting on opposite sides of a decision, still capable of honesty.

"Conviction is slower," Michael added.

David nodded. The sentence was simple and true and it carried no judgment. It was an observation from a man who had chosen a different path and could see, from that vantage point, what David's path cost.

Driving back to the office, David felt neither vindicated nor discouraged.

He felt the absence of inherited momentum.

It was a specific feeling—not emptiness, but lightness. The lightness of a structure that carries no accumulated weight. No legacy referral patterns. No automatic revenue from market appreciation. No compounding pipeline from institutional reputation. Just the work itself, stripped of everything that had once surrounded it.

Back at the walnut table that afternoon, he opened the projection spreadsheet again.

The firm would survive.

But survival was not the same as growth.

He looked around the room—the proportionate office, the local art, the chairs selected carefully, the wood that anchored the space. Everything reflected alignment. Every surface, every choice, every detail communicated what the firm believed and how it intended to practice.

Nothing guaranteed expansion.

For the first time since drawing the line with Michael, doubt rose clearly.

Not doubt about leaving. He did not regret the decision. He did not wish himself back into the conference room at Northbridge, reviewing recap projections under institutional benchmarks. The question was not whether he had been right to leave.

It was doubt about building.

Doubt about whether alignment, however principled, was sufficient to sustain a practice over years. Whether clarity, however earned, could generate the relationships and revenue necessary to endure. Whether the thing he had built—beautiful, proportionate, honest—would attract the clients it deserved, or whether it would remain a monument to conviction visited by too few people to justify its existence.

And doubt, he knew, is the natural companion of any decision made without a safety net.

He closed the laptop and sat quietly in the fading light. The walnut table held the warmth of the day's sun. The room was still. The building was emptying around him with the quiet rhythm of an ordinary evening.

If growth was no longer weather, then it would have to be cultivated.

The question was whether he had the patience to cultivate it.

Chapter 19

Return

Thomas did not schedule the visit.

Rachel stepped into David's office late on a Thursday afternoon in September and stood just inside the doorway. She held no folder, carried no message. Her posture alone carried the information.

"Thomas is here," she said.

There was no added tone to her voice. No inflection of surprise, no signal beyond the fact itself. But Rachel had been with David long enough to understand the weight of certain names. Thomas was one of them.

David stood immediately.

He did not rush. But he did not pause, either.

Thomas was in the conference room, standing beside the walnut table. He was not seated. He was running his hand slowly across the surface as if reacquainting himself with something familiar—something he had once helped bring into being and then stepped away from.

"It's holding up," Thomas said without turning around.

"Yes," David replied.

Thomas stepped back and studied the table from a slight distance, then glanced around the room. His eyes lingered on the artwork, the trim, the way the light settled across the floor in the late afternoon. He seemed to be measuring the space not for size or decoration, but for something harder to name. Coherence, maybe. Or stillness.

"It feels different," he said.

"How?" David asked.

Thomas considered the question the way he considered most things—without hurry, without performance.

"Quieter," he said finally. "Deliberate."

They sat across from one another at the round table. No head. No hierarchy. The geometry of the table made that impossible, and David had long since stopped thinking of that as incidental. It was the point.

"I've been watching," Thomas said.

David did not respond. He had learned, through Harry and through his own slow education, that silence after a statement like that was not avoidance. It was invitation.

"I assumed there would be announcements," Thomas continued. "Marketing pushes. Positioning. Some version of the growth story dressed in new language."

"There weren't," David said.

"No," Thomas agreed. "There weren't."

Silence settled between them—not uncomfortable, but evaluative. It was the kind of silence that only exists between people who have shared enough history to let the room hold what words would cheapen.

"I needed to see if this was reaction or conviction," Thomas said at last.

David felt the weight of that sentence settle over him without defensiveness. It was a fair test. Perhaps the only fair test. Anyone could leave a firm in frustration. The question was whether what followed the leaving was built from principle or from wound.

"And?" he asked.

Thomas looked down at the wood grain beneath his hand. He traced a ring in the walnut with his finger, the way someone might trace the outline of a thought still forming.

"I left because Northbridge began to feel larger than the relationship," he said. "I didn't want to be absorbed into scale. I wanted discernment. I wanted to sit across from someone who was thinking about my situation—not managing a portfolio that happened to have my name on it."

David remained still. He did not defend. He did not explain what Northbridge had become or why. Thomas was not asking for that. He was telling his own story, and it deserved the dignity of being heard without correction.

"I didn't follow immediately because I needed to see if this would become another version of growth dressed differently," Thomas continued. "There are firms that change their name and their brochure and call it transformation. I needed to see if this was that."

"And what did you see?" David asked quietly.

"I saw restraint," Thomas replied. "I saw you not pushing. Not calling. Not positioning. I saw you build something and then wait for it to speak for itself."

He paused.

"And I saw you buy this table after I said not yet. That mattered."

David did not speak. The table had been a risk. A significant expenditure in a season of uncertainty, built from a conversation with a man who had declined to follow him. Claire had understood it. Harry had affirmed it without saying so directly. But hearing Thomas name it—hearing him say that mattered—was something David had not anticipated feeling so deeply.

"I'm ready," Thomas said.

The words did not arrive with flourish. They did not arrive with conditions or caveats or the careful hedging of a man protecting his optionality.

They arrived with finality.

"You're sure?" David asked.

"Yes."

They discussed logistics calmly. Custodial transfer timing. Planning updates. Coordination with Thomas's CPA and estate attorney. The mechanics of reunification, handled with the same care and precision that had characterized the separation. There was no urgency, because urgency would have contradicted everything that had brought Thomas back to this room.

There was no handshake sealing victory. No celebratory tone. What passed between them was quieter than that—a mutual recognition that something had been tested and had held.

When Thomas stood to leave, he paused at the doorway. He turned back and looked at the room one more time—the table, the light, the deliberate stillness of a firm that had chosen proportion over momentum.

"This doesn't feel bigger," he said. "It feels truer."

After he left, David remained seated at the table. He did not stand to watch Thomas walk down the hall. He did not reach for his phone. He sat with the weight of what had just happened and let it settle without rushing to interpret it.

The doubt had not vanished entirely. It never would. David understood that now. Doubt was not the enemy of conviction. It was the companion that kept conviction honest.

But it had shifted. The doubt no longer asked whether he had made the right decision. It asked only whether he was continuing to honor it.

Thomas had not returned because he was persuaded by marketing or momentum. He had not returned because of a compelling pitch or a favorable fee schedule. He had returned because he had observed congruence—between what David said and what David did, between the firm's stated values and its lived behavior—over a period of time long enough to test it.

That is what alignment produces. Not speed. Not scale. Trust that has been earned through restraint.

David picked up his phone and called Harry.

"He came back," he said.

Harry did not respond immediately. David had come to expect that. Harry's silences were never empty. They were the space where the real conversation was being assembled.

"And?" he asked.

"He said it feels smaller," David replied. "But truer."

There was a pause on the other end of the line. David could almost hear Harry smiling.

"And who does Thomas know?" Harry asked.

The question landed differently now. Not as tactic. Not as strategy. Not as the opening move in some client acquisition framework.

As stewardship.

David looked around the room. The walnut table. The light settling into its afternoon angle. The quiet hum of a firm that had chosen to grow by depth rather than by reach.

Thomas was not simply a returning client. He was not a recovered asset or a vindication of David's decision to leave. He was a node in a network of craftsmen, founders, disciplined operators—people who valued deliberation over spectacle, substance over signal. The kind of people who noticed restraint precisely because so few firms practiced it.

Alignment was not self-contained. It did not stop at the boundaries of the firm or the edges of the financial plan.

It was relational. It radiated outward through the people it served, into the communities and families and businesses they touched.

After he ended the call, David remained seated a while longer. The room was quiet. Rachel had gone home. The building had settled into its evening stillness.

The firm had not surged. It had not exploded into the market with the force of a compelling narrative or a viral strategy.

But it had anchored.

And anchoring, David realized, precedes growth. Not the growth the industry celebrates—the kind measured in basis points and headcount and press mentions. But the kind that endures. The kind built slowly, deliberately, through relationships that have been tested by patience and proven by time.

Chapter 20

Cultivation

Thomas's return did not produce an immediate surge in new business.

What it produced was clarity.

David understood now—not as theory but as lived experience—that if growth was going to come, it would not arrive through weather. It would not be inherited from market appreciation or brand momentum or the passive drift of assets compounding under a familiar logo. It would have to be cultivated deliberately, through relationships that reflected the same posture he was trying to embody. The word mattered to him. Cultivation implied patience. It implied tending. It implied that what you were growing had a nature of its own, and your job was not to force it but to create conditions where it could thrive.

The shift began quietly.

He called Andrew Bell, a valuation specialist he had known for years but had never elevated beyond occasional collaboration. Andrew was careful and methodical, the kind of professional who asked more questions than he answered. His reports were dense, built from first principles rather than templates. His style was understated. He had never chased scale aggressively, and that restraint had cost him visibility in a market that rewarded volume. David had always respected him. He had simply never acted on that respect with intention.

"This isn't about a transaction," David said when Andrew answered.

"That's unusual," Andrew replied.

"I have two clients who will likely face liquidity events in the next couple of years," David continued. "I'd like you to meet them before they need you."

There was a brief silence on the line. David could feel Andrew recalibrating. In their industry, introductions were almost always transactional—offered with an expectation of reciprocity, structured around mutual benefit. What David was describing was different. He was offering access without conditions.

"You're not requesting a proposal?" Andrew asked.

"No."

"You're not asking me to pitch?"

"No."

"Then what are you asking?"

"Conversation," David said. "Without agenda."

Andrew came to the office two weeks later.

Thomas happened to be there that afternoon reviewing updated planning documents. David invited him to join them—not to perform any function, but because the conversation would be richer for his presence. Thomas understood transitions. He had lived through the tension of holding something you built while also letting it evolve.

The three men sat at the walnut table. No slides were prepared. No formal presentation materials were distributed. The conversation began with questions about timing, family governance, and the psychological impact of selling a company that had defined identity for decades. These were not financial planning questions. They were human questions—the kind that most advisors scheduled for the end of the process, if they addressed them at all.

At one point, Andrew began outlining valuation methodologies in technical detail. He was thorough and precise, and David could see that his instinct was to demonstrate competence through depth of analysis. David listened for a moment before gently redirecting the conversation.

"Before we optimize," he said, "what problem are we solving?"

The question shifted the posture of the room. Andrew paused. Thomas leaned forward slightly. The discussion moved away from multiples and toward purpose. Toward what the founder actually wanted life to look like after liquidity. Toward what mattered beyond the spreadsheet.

This is what a consultant does. A technician optimizes the answer. A consultant reframes the question.

When Andrew left, Thomas remained seated.

"You didn't need anything from that," he said.

"No," David replied.

"You weren't positioning him."

"No."

Thomas ran his hand along the table—a gesture that had become his signature in that room, the way some people tap a desk or fidget with a pen. For Thomas, touching the walnut was something closer to grounding.

"That's rare," he said.

The pattern continued.

Rachel organized a small breakfast one morning in the conference room. Four clients. Two professional collaborators. Eight chairs around the round table—every seat occupied, no one at the head, because there was no head to occupy.

There was no banner. No program name. No structured agenda distributed in advance. No branded materials or takeaway folders.

The invitation had been simple:

Conversation about transition timing. No presentation.

When the morning arrived, David opened with a question rather than a statement.

"What surprised you most when you stepped away from day-to-day operations?" he asked one of the founders present.

The discussion unfolded without choreography. One client admitted he had underestimated how disorienting unstructured time would feel—that after decades of being needed, the sudden absence of obligation was not freedom but vertigo. Another spoke about the unexpected strain liquidity placed on extended family relationships, how money that was supposed to simplify things had instead surfaced tensions that had been dormant for years. A CPA described how tax strategy sometimes overshadowed relational consequence, how he had seen families optimize their way into estrangement.

At one point, a banker began outlining a financing structure that could increase after-tax yield. He was articulate and well-prepared, and the numbers were compelling. David listened and then asked quietly, "Before we refine yield, what are we preserving?"

The tone of the room shifted again. The banker paused. The question was not adversarial. It was clarifying. And it reoriented the entire conversation toward something the room could feel but had not yet named.

After the breakfast, one of the clients lingered. He stood near the window, looking out at the parking lot as if deciding whether to say something.

"I've never been in a room like that," he said.

"How so?" David asked.

"No one was trying to win."

Rachel began tracking introductions differently after that morning.

Not in terms of projected revenue. Not in terms of assets under management or estimated wallet share or any of the metrics the industry used to quantify the value of a relationship before the relationship had even begun.

In terms of posture.

Which clients invited counsel early? Which professionals asked questions before offering solutions? Which conversations felt collaborative rather than competitive? She was mapping the relational topology of the firm—not its financial footprint but its gravitational field.

Thomas introduced David to a commercial banker who preferred disciplined manufacturers to venture-backed startups. The banker, in turn, introduced a founder who valued deliberation over speed. That founder mentioned David to his estate attorney, who had been looking for an advisor willing to sit in complexity rather than simplify it away.

The introductions did not create sudden acceleration.

They created depth.

Each new relationship arrived not because David had asked for it, but because someone who had experienced his posture believed it would serve someone they cared about. That was the mechanism. Not referral as transaction. Referral as extension of trust.

One afternoon, reviewing quarterly numbers, Rachel looked up from her laptop.

"We're not bigger," she said.

"No," David replied.

"But we're not dependent on weather either."

He understood what she meant. The firm's growth was no longer a function of market movement or inherited momentum. It was no longer accidental.

It was relational.

It emerged from being received.

Three months after Thomas returned, he brought a friend.

They sat again at the walnut table—Thomas in the chair he had begun to think of as his, though he would never have said so. His friend was a manufacturing executive, deliberate in speech, skeptical by temperament. The kind of person who evaluated everything twice before committing once.

"This is the table I told you about," Thomas said, resting his hand lightly on the wood.

His friend looked around the room and smiled.

"You're selling furniture now?" he asked.

Thomas shook his head.

"No. I'm showing you how he builds."

The conversation that followed was patient. There was no closing language. No positioning. No trial close or soft commitment or any of the choreography the industry trained advisors to deploy. Only questions about purpose, timing, and consequence. Only the kind of conversation that happens when no one in the room is performing.

Two weeks later, the friend moved his accounts.

There was no announcement. No celebratory email. No internal memo marking the win.

Just onboarding. Careful, thorough, deliberate onboarding—the kind that treated the beginning of a relationship with the same seriousness as its continuation.

That evening, David called Harry.

"It's working," he said.

Harry was quiet for a moment.

"What's working?" he asked.

David looked around the conference room. The table. The chairs. The light settling into its evening angle. The faint impressions left by the hands and coffee cups and conversations of people who had chosen to be there.

"Building where I'm received," he said.

There was a pause.

"It's slower," David added.

"Yes," Harry replied.

"It's narrower."

"Yes."

"It's peaceful."

Harry's voice softened. David could hear something in it that he had not heard before—not pride exactly, but recognition. The recognition of a teacher watching a student arrive at something that cannot be taught, only discovered.

"That's because you stopped protecting," he said. "And started stewarding."

David did not answer immediately. He let the distinction settle. Protecting was about fear—holding what you had, defending against loss, building walls around what felt fragile. Stewarding was about faithfulness—tending what had been entrusted to you, not because it was yours, but because you had been given responsibility for its care.

He had not left for speed.

He had left for alignment.

And alignment, he was learning, created its own gravity. Not the loud, pulling gravity of scale and ambition. The quiet gravity of congruence—the kind that drew people not because they were persuaded, but because they recognized something true.

Chapter 21

The Table

Harry arrived on a quiet Thursday afternoon in early autumn. The firm was still young enough that its rhythms had not fully settled. There were no awards on the walls. No framed press clippings. No sense of institutional permanence that comes from decades of accumulated history and carefully curated reputation. The reception area was orderly and warm, but it carried none of the accumulated gravity that Northbridge once had. It carried, instead, something lighter—an openness that David had not anticipated. The absence of legacy was not emptiness. It was possibility.

Rachel had left early to attend her son's school event. The building was nearly empty. David was alone in a way that would have unsettled him six months ago but now felt like the natural rhythm of a practice built at human scale.

David met Harry at the entrance and walked him down the hallway toward the conference room. They did not speak as they walked. Harry moved slowly, taking in the space—the artwork, the light, the quiet that saturated the building like something chosen rather than accidental.

When they stepped inside, Harry stopped.

The walnut table sat solidly in the center of the room, catching the angled afternoon light. Its grain had deepened slightly since installation, the surface already carrying faint marks from coffee cups and resting hands. It had acquired, in just a few months, the patina of use—the evidence that something had happened here. That conversations had been held. That decisions had been weighed. That people had sat in this room and spoken truthfully about things that mattered.

"So this is it," Harry said quietly.

"It's just wood," David replied.

Harry stepped forward and placed his palm on the surface. He held it there for a moment, the way someone might place a hand on the shoulder of a person they were proud of.

"No," he said gently. "It isn't."

They sat across from one another. No head of the table. No dominant position. The geometry enforced equality, and Harry seemed to notice this immediately—his eyes tracing the circle before he settled into his chair.

For several moments neither of them spoke. The room held their silence without pressing them to fill it.

"How long has it been?" Harry asked.

"Just over six months," David replied.

"And?"

David leaned back slightly in his chair. He considered the question not as small talk but as what it was—an invitation to account.

"It's smaller," he said.

Harry nodded.

"Yes."

"It's narrower," David continued.

"Yes."

"It's quieter."

Harry waited. He did not fill the space. He did not offer reassurance or reframe the observation into something more optimistic. He simply waited, because he understood that David was not listing deficiencies. He was arriving somewhere.

"But it's aligned," David finished.

The word did not carry bravado. It carried relief. The relief of a man who had made a costly decision and discovered, on the other side of it, that the cost had purchased something real.

Harry studied him carefully.

"You're not proven yet," he said.

"No."

"You're not scaling aggressively."

"No."

"You're not maximizing leverage."

David smiled faintly.

"No."

Harry leaned forward slightly.

"But you're settled."

David let that word settle inside him before responding. Settled. Not triumphant. Not vindicated. Not proven. Settled. It was a word that carried no applause and needed none.

"Yes."

He had expected courage to feel larger when it finally materialized. He had expected some sense of expansion, perhaps even vindication—a moment when the industry would see what he had done and recognize it as bold or visionary. Instead, it had felt like exposure followed by stillness. Like stepping out of a building you had lived in for years and finding that the air outside was not warmer or colder. It was simply clearer.

"I thought leaving would prove something," David admitted. "That growth would validate the decision. That the numbers would demonstrate that I was right."

"And has it?" Harry asked.

"Not dramatically," David said. "It's growing, but not exponentially. It's growing relationally. One conversation at a time. One introduction at a time. One person recognizing something in this firm that they had been looking for without knowing how to name it."

Harry nodded.

"That's different," he said.

David rested his hands lightly on the table.

"I had to confront something honestly," he continued. "I wasn't afraid of recap. I wasn't afraid of capital. I wasn't even afraid of the structural changes that would follow. I was afraid of misalignment."

Harry said nothing. His silence was not absence. It was the kind of presence that gave permission for whatever came next.

"For years," David went on, "I told myself that as long as I was serving clients faithfully, structure didn't matter as much. That I could maintain my convictions inside any framework if I was disciplined enough. But it does matter. Incentives shape posture. Compensation shapes behavior. Growth assumptions shape conversation. And if clients trust me for judgment—if that is the actual asset I am offering—then the structure I operate within has to make that judgment possible. Not just tolerable. Central."

He paused. The room was quiet enough that he could hear the faint hum of the building's climate system, steady and unobtrusive—the way infrastructure should be.

"And if clients trust me for judgment, then the structure I operate within has to make that clear. Not as marketing language. As lived reality."

Harry's voice softened.

"And why does that matter so much to you?" he asked.

David did not answer immediately.

He looked down at the table, at the circular grain that carried no head, no hierarchy. At the marks left by the hands of people who had sat here and spoken about what they valued. Thomas. Rachel. Andrew. The founders who had lingered after the breakfast and said things they had not said in rooms designed to impress them.

"Because my work is not neutral," he said at last. "It isn't just financial optimization. It isn't just asset management dressed in better language. It affects families. It affects legacy. It affects how people steward what they've been given—not just their wealth but their time, their influence, their responsibility to the people who come after them."

He lifted his eyes.

"And I believe that calling comes from somewhere specific."

Harry held his gaze. The room was entirely still.

"Say it," he said gently.

David felt no hesitation now. There had been a time—years, perhaps—when he would have softened this. When he would have spoken in the language of values or purpose or meaning, which were true enough but incomplete. He would have framed his conviction in terms the industry could receive without discomfort. But that time had passed. The decision to leave had stripped away the need for translation.

"I believe it comes from Jesus Christ," he said plainly. "Not from market forces. Not from professional ambition. Not from identity tied to scale. From Him."

The room was still.

"For a while," David continued, "I tried to frame this as strategic evolution. As professional positioning. As a sophisticated response to structural change in the industry. But that wasn't honest. It was obedience."

The word landed in the room the way it always did when spoken with sincerity—without apology, without performance, without the need for the listener to agree or be persuaded.

Harry's eyes glistened slightly, though his voice remained steady.

"When we first spoke about Luke 10," he said, "you were wrestling with direction. You were trying to reconcile conviction with pragmatism. Christ didn't send them out to maximize coverage. He didn't send them with a strategy for scale. He sent them to speak peace and stay where they were received."

David nodded.

"I built scale where I was effective," he said. "Now I'm building depth where I'm received."

The distinction was not subtle. It was the hinge of everything.

"And what did it cost?" Harry asked.

"Reputation," David said. "Momentum. Predictability. The comfort of knowing that the path was mapped and the outcomes were modeled."

"And what did it give you?"

David looked around the room. The walnut table. The afternoon light. The quiet hum of a firm that had chosen depth over reach, alignment over acceleration, obedience over optimization.

"Peace."

Harry leaned back slowly.

"Peace isn't the goal," he said. "It's the fruit."

They sat in silence for a long moment. It was the kind of silence that exists between two people who have arrived at the same understanding from different directions—one through decades of wisdom, the other through the costly education of lived experience.

"I need you to understand something," Harry added quietly. "When you called me months ago, I sensed that this wasn't about dissatisfaction. It wasn't about frustration with a partner or resistance to change. It was about stewardship. Many successful men talk about purpose. They reference it in marketing materials and keynote addresses and year-end letters to clients. Few are willing to risk comfort for obedience."

David felt the weight of that statement without pride. Pride would have contradicted it.

"I didn't feel brave," he said.

"Courage rarely feels dramatic," Harry replied. "It feels costly. It feels quiet. It feels like sitting alone in a conference room wondering if you've made the biggest mistake of your career."

David traced the edge of the table lightly.

"I'm not trying to build something smaller," he said. "I'm trying to build something truer."

Harry smiled faintly—the first full smile David had seen from him in this room.

"And clarity attracts the right people," he said. "Not all people. Not the most people. The right people."

They rose from the table together.

As Harry reached the doorway, he paused. He turned back one last time, and David saw something in his expression that he could not quite name—something between gratitude and completion, as if this visit had closed a circle Harry had been drawing for longer than David knew.

"You built the firm you would build today," he said.

David looked back at the room.

"It's still forming," he replied.

"It always will be," Harry said.

When the door closed behind him, David returned to the table and sat alone for a few minutes. The light had shifted while they spoke. The afternoon was tilting toward evening, and the walnut grain caught the lower angle in a way that deepened its color, made it warmer.

He did not feel triumphant.

He did not feel vindicated.

He felt aligned.

Courage had not guaranteed scale. It had not produced the kind of growth the industry celebrates or the kind of story conference speakers tell to thunderous applause. It had not made him famous or wealthy beyond what he had been before.

It had required obedience.

And obedience had produced peace.

Not the peace of certainty. Not the peace of having every question answered or every outcome secured. The peace of knowing that what he had built, and how he had built it, and why he had built it, were finally the same answer.

Chapter 22

If You Were Starting Today

If you have stayed with this story to the end, then you already understand that it is not primarily about recapitalization. It is not about private equity. It is not even about leaving a firm.

It is about a question that becomes unavoidable once it is honestly formed.

If you were starting today, would you build the firm you are currently running?

That question does not carry accusation. It carries clarity. And clarity, when everything is working, can be more disruptive than crisis.

Most of the advisors who will read this book are not struggling. They are not in decline. They are not scrambling to survive. They have built real enterprises. They have teams. They have loyal clients. They have margin. Many have enterprise value that earlier generations of advisors could hardly have imagined.

Nothing appears to be broken.

And that is precisely why the question matters.

When firms are in distress, change is forced. The market removes options. Revenue compression narrows choices. Departures expose fragility. In those seasons, adaptation is reactive. You do not choose clarity. Clarity chooses you.

But when everything works—when growth is steady, retention is high, and recruiting conversations are active—clarity becomes voluntary. No one is forcing you to reconsider structure. No one is demanding reexamination. You can continue operating successfully for years, perhaps decades, without confronting deeper alignment.

That is where courage becomes necessary. Not the courage of desperation, but the courage of honesty. The willingness to ask a question whose answer might cost you something.

Years ago, I wrote *Can I Borrow Your Car?* because I believed something essential had been diluted in our profession. Too many financial advisors were competing on performance, product access, and personality. They were refining tactics while neglecting the asset that actually separated them from software and commoditized investment management.

That asset was trust.

I wrote that book to remind advisors that when a client metaphorically hands you the keys to something they value, they are not purchasing a return stream. They are extending belief. They are entrusting you with judgment. They are placing their future in your discernment.

Trust is not built through projection output. It is not built through polished reviews or quarterly presentations or any of the performance rituals our industry has developed to simulate competence. It is built through the consistent exercise of judgment on behalf of another person—in moments that cannot be automated, in conversations that cannot be scripted, in decisions that carry weight precisely because they require a human being who has earned the right to be heard.

That message resonated with many of you because you knew it was true. You had experienced it. The deepest client relationships in your firm were not anchored in asset allocation. They were anchored in discernment. In timing. In counsel offered at moments that could not be solved by spreadsheets alone.

But over time, another realization surfaced for me.

If trust and judgment are the true foundation of this profession, then structure cannot remain secondary. You cannot preach judgment while compensating yourself primarily for exposure. You cannot emphasize discernment while designing growth models that assume accumulation as the default outcome. You cannot claim to value trust while allowing referrals to occur randomly and hoping market appreciation fills your revenue gaps.

At some point, the firm itself must reflect what you say you believe.

This book became necessary because the environment around us has changed in ways that make that reflection unavoidable.

Technology has isolated calculation. Planning tools that once required teams can now be accessed inexpensively. Investment management has become broadly available. Transparency around fees and performance is increasing. Clients can see what math costs. They can compare it. They can replace it.

What they cannot replicate is judgment.

Judgment is not a chart. It is not a Monte Carlo simulation. It is not a rebalancing algorithm or a risk tolerance questionnaire or a model portfolio assigned by age.

Judgment is the conversation that prevents a founder from signing a document when fatigue clouds clarity. It is the counsel that slows liquidity long enough to consider family dynamics. It is the restraint that protects governance before it protects yield. It is the willingness to say "not yet" when everyone else in the room is saying "now."

If that is what your clients ultimately trust you for, then your structure must make that obvious. Not eventually. Not aspirationally. Now.

I am not here to tell you what your answer should be.

That distinction matters to me, and I want to be direct about it. This book is not a prescription. It is not a blueprint for how to restructure your firm or a manifesto against any particular business model. It's not my intent to tell you that your path should look like David's, or like mine, or like anyone else's.

What I am offering is something I believe is more valuable than a prescription. I am offering you a framework for thinking—a set of questions worth sitting with long before the industry forces you to answer them in a hurry.

Because here is what I have observed, sitting across the table from advisors for years: The ones who navigate change well are not the ones who had the best strategy. They are the ones who had done the interior work early. They had already asked themselves what mattered. They had already examined what they were building and why. They had already confronted the distance—if there was any—between their convictions and their compensation, between their values and their structure, between the practice they described to clients and the business they were actually running.

When change arrived—and it always arrives—they were not starting from scratch. They were building from alignment.

That is what I want for you. Not a decision made under pressure, but a framework built in peace.

The questions are not complicated. But they require honesty.

What do you actually believe about the work you do? Is it optimization, or is it something deeper? Is it a service you provide, or is it a calling you steward?

How does growth arrive in your firm? Is it cultivated through relationships that reflect your values, or does it accumulate passively through market movement and inherited momentum? Do you know the difference? Does your team?

What does your compensation model reward? Does it reward the exercise of judgment, or does it reward the accumulation of exposure? Are those the same thing in your firm, or have they quietly diverged?

Who are your clients becoming under your counsel? Are they more deliberate? More aligned with their own values? More prepared for the decisions that wealth eventually forces? Or are they simply wealthier?

If the answer to that last question gives you pause, you are not alone. And the pause itself is valuable. It is the beginning of the framework.

You can build scale where you are effective. Many have done so with discipline and integrity. There is nothing inherently wrong with scale. Some of the most principled advisors I know operate large, institutional firms with genuine conviction.

Or you can build depth where you are received. You can cultivate a firm designed around discernment, around being invited early rather than consulted late, around compensation that reflects counsel rather than exposure.

Both paths require skill. Both require sacrifice. But they are not identical. One optimizes for velocity. The other optimizes for congruence. And only you can determine which one reflects what you actually believe about the work.

For me, this is not merely strategic. It is spiritual.

I do not believe my work is neutral. I do not believe financial advice is simply optimization dressed in professional language. I believe it is stewardship. I believe my calling as a coach is accountable to Jesus Christ. That conviction shapes how I think about money, growth, reputation, and risk. It shapes how I think about courage. It shapes what I am willing to build and what I am willing to walk away from.

Courage, in this context, is not loud. It does not announce itself publicly. It is often misunderstood. It can look like unnecessary disruption to those who value stability above alignment. It can look like foolishness to those who measure success primarily in scale.

But obedience produces something that scale cannot guarantee.

It produces peace.

You may articulate your foundation differently. You may not use the same language I do. You may arrive at your convictions through philosophy, through experience, through the accumulated wisdom of watching what endures and what does not. But you must have a foundation. You must know what it is. And you must be willing to let it shape your structure, not just your marketing.

Because the era we are entering will not reward vagueness. It will separate firms that are structurally aligned from those that are merely historically successful. The firms that thrive will not necessarily be the largest or the most operationally efficient. They will be the ones whose structure and posture and compensation and growth all point in the same direction—toward a conviction that the founder was willing to name.

Some firms will grow larger and more institutional. Some will refine operational leverage and build extraordinary enterprise value. Some will narrow and deepen, cultivating clients who invite counsel before acting. Some will continue without asking the question at all.

The future of financial advice does not belong exclusively to any one model.

But it will belong to those who are aligned.

Many of you reading this have earned optionality. Years of disciplined work have given you liquidity, leverage, and reputation. You can secure comfort if you choose to. You can solidify structure and move confidently into the next decade without revisiting foundational assumptions.

Optionality is a gift.

It is also a test.

You can use it to protect comfort.

Or you can use it to protect congruence.

This book is not asking you to leave your firm. It is not prescribing recap or rejecting it. It is not romanticizing independence or condemning scale.

It is asking you to do something harder than any of those things.

It is asking you to sit with the question long enough to let it do its work. To resist the impulse to answer quickly or defensively or strategically. To let the question settle into the quiet places where you already know what you believe but have not yet given yourself permission to act on it.

If you were starting today, would you build this?

If the answer is yes, then build it more deliberately and with greater clarity. Name what you believe. Let your structure testify to it. Let your clients see it in how you grow, how you hire, how you compensate, how you spend your time.

If the answer is no, then you have an extraordinary opportunity. Not a crisis. An opportunity. The opportunity to begin building—from alignment, in your own time, on your own terms—the firm that reflects what you have always believed but never fully expressed in structure.

That is what taking your time provides. Not delay. Not avoidance. The chance to think clearly about what matters before the market or a partner or an outside capital event forces the question on someone else's timeline.

Courage rarely feels dramatic. It feels costly. It often feels slower than you would prefer.

But alignment produces something rare in professional life.

Peace.

Not the peace of having every answer. Not the peace of certainty or market dominance or industry recognition.

The peace of congruence.

Build the firm you would build today.

Dedication & Acknowledgment

This book exists because people believed in it before it was written and because people believed in me when I was still learning what I had to say.

To my wife, Jocelyn. You have seen every version of me, including the ones I would rather forget, and you have stayed. Not out of obligation, but out of a love I did not earn and still do not fully deserve. You are the steadiest person I know, and your faith in Christ has shaped mine more than any sermon ever could. I love you.

To my mom, Dawn. You taught me to read, to write, and to be curious about other people: three gifts that explain most of what I do for a living. Your belief in me has never wavered, even when the evidence was thin. You are still the first person who showed me what authenticity looks like. You are the most natural networker I know, and I carry that with me into every conversation I have.

To my son, Robert. Your joy is unearned by circumstance and undimmed by difficulty, and it rebukes every excuse I have ever made about why something was too hard. You teach me humility every day without saying a word. I love you, Son.

To my late father, Bill. You told me to remember who I am, and I am still trying to live up to that. You were the better writer between us, and I feel your absence every time I sit down to work on something like this, or when I step into a beautiful mountain stream to fly fish. I miss you.

To my clients, past and present. You are the reason I do this work. Your courage to confront what is comfortable in pursuit of what is congruent is the heartbeat of this book. I will always be honored that you call me "Coach."

To Scott Snider and the Exit Planning Institute. Scott, your belief in *Can I Borrow Your Car?* opened doors I had not imagined: inviting me onto the faculty of the online academy and onto the stage at the Exit Planning Summit. Your vision for exit planning across the world has given practitioners like me a framework and a community, and I am grateful for the opportunity to be part of what you are building.

To George Sandmann and Growth Drive. George, you are one of my closest friends in this work, and you have taught me more about what it means to be a practitioner, not just a thinker, but someone who drives real growth inside real companies, than I can properly credit in a paragraph. Your methodology has sharpened how I serve, and your friendship has deepened how I think.

To Tina Corner Stolz and LX Council. Tina, you are a force. Your excellence in business is matched only by your generosity in partnership. You have collaborated with me, mentored me, and challenged me to be better in ways that have quietly shaped the ideas in these pages. I am grateful for your friendship and your example.

To you, the reader. You picked up this book, which means you are willing to sit with a question that most people avoid. Do not let the momentum of what is working keep you from asking whether it is what you would build. You deserve that clarity.

And to my Lord and Savior, Jesus Christ. If there is anything true and lasting in these pages, it comes from you. The rest is mine, and I am grateful that your grace does not require me to be perfect—only willing. I hope this book serves your purposes more than my own.

www.ingramcontent.com/pod-product-compliance
Lightning Source LLC
LaVergne TN
LVHW010616100826
845148LV00014B/2995